Dedicated to the long life and flourishing activity of His Holiness the Seventeenth Gyalwang Karmapa, Ogyen Trinley Dorje

THE SEVENTEENTH GYALWANG
KARMAPA, OGYEN TRINLEY DORJE

FREEDOM
THROUGH MEDITATION

Translators
David Karma Choephel
Tyler Dewar
Michele Martin (and editor)

KTD Publications
Woodstock, New York

Published in 2018 by
KTD Publications
335 Meads Mountain Road
Woodstock, NY 12498, USA
www.KTDPublications.org

Freedom through Meditation
The Seventeenth Gyalwang Karmapa, Ogyen Trinley Dorje
Translators:
David Karma Choephel
Tyler Dewar
Michele Martin (and editor)
Cover design by Maureen McNicholas
Front cover photo of Karmapa by Robert Hansen-Sturm

ISBN: 978-1-934608-57-9
Library of Congress Control Number: 2018949003

This book is printed in the United States on acid-free, 100% PCR,
FSC Recycled Certified paper. See Environmental Impact
Statement p. 146

Contents

Preface
The Seventeenth Gyalwang Karmapa Ogyen Trinley Dorje

In the summer of 2017, I was fortunate to be able to visit Canada for the very first time, traveling the breadth of this vast land to Toronto, Montreal, Ottawa, Edmonton, Calgary, and Vancouver. In so doing, I was following in the footsteps of the Sixteenth Gyalwang Karmapa, Rangjung Rigpe Dorje, who visited Canada in the 1970s. I had the chance to see for myself the places where he had been. It gave me great joy to witness how the foundations he had laid so many years ago for the flourishing of the Buddhist Dharma have been preserved into the twenty-first century.

One of my principal aims in visiting Canada was to meet with the Tibetan diaspora, especially in Toronto, which is the largest Tibetan community in North America. I was also delighted to have a chance to visit many of the Dharma centers, where I met and talked with members, gave teachings and empowerments, and was able to deepen Dharmic connections with students. The itinerary included several public events such as meetings with

Canadian parliamentarians in Ottawa and the state legislature of Ontario, a dialogue with Buddhists from other traditions, and a discussion with Professor Wade Davis at the University of British Columbia in Vancouver, and it also gave me the opportunity to meet with representatives of the First Nations.

My impression is that Canada is a truly multicultural society. Throughout my stay in Canada, I observed the tolerance and respect with which the different peoples treat each other's cultural and religious traditions. In my view, this is the reason why Canadian people from so many different backgrounds can live and work together in harmony and has proven a very supportive environment for Tibetans and Tibetan culture.

I would like to thank Khenpo David Karma Choephel and Tyler Dewar, who were my translators on the tour and whose translations provided the basis for this book, *Freedom through Meditation*. Finally, I would like to thank Michele Martin. This book would not have existed without her dedicated effort in translating, checking, and editing the compilation. I welcome its publication and hope that it will be of interest and bring benefit to many.

The Seventeenth Karmapa, Ogyen Trinley Dorje
June 18, 2018

Introduction

For one historic month, from May 29 to June 29, 2017, His Holiness the Seventeenth Karmapa traveled and taught throughout Canada for the first time. From another perspective, however, this was a return visit after a forty-year absence, for he was following the path of his predecessor, the Sixteenth Karmapa, Rangjung Rigpe Dorje, who had made teaching tours to Canada in 1974, 1977, and 1980. This time the Karmapa visited Toronto, Montreal, Ottawa, Edmonton, Calgary, and Vancouver. Wherever he stopped, he met with large groups of Tibetans who were delighted to welcome him to the multicultural world of Canada. Attuned to our present world, he gave teachings that covered the environment, social responsibility, working with our afflictions, and instructions on how to meditate. He visited parliament and engaged in lively dialogs with monks from the Theravadin and Mahayana traditions as well as a professor from the University of British Columbia. The Karmapa also offered five empowerments, met with three major Tibetan communities in Toronto, Calgary, and Vancouver plus MPs from the Legislative Assembly of Ontario, and blessed temples and Dharma centers of various traditions.

The eleven teachings selected for this volume represent his major talks and excerpts from an empowerment. Taken as a whole, they give all the elements needed for a fulfilling Dharma practice, from the panorama of the entire path, to subtle teachings on working with all aspects of our minds and emotions while also giving heartfelt encouragement to take the path of compassion and engage in activities that benefit others. Throughout his talks, the Karmapa pointed to the interconnection between meditation and social involvement: in the seventh chapter he links mindfulness to taking responsibility for the environment, and in the last chapter he responds with an open heart to specific questions about meditation and practice in the world.

The Karmapa's style of teaching is unique, and a few comments might be helpful to illustrate a deeper level meaning, so we are not mislead by what appears closer to the surface. In Tibetan writing, there is something that could be called a literary device, which is known as "rejecting arrogance" or "humility" (*kengpa pongwa, khengs pa spong ba*). In this mode authors deflate any chance of being puffed up about their positive qualities. One of the most famous examples can be found in the *Thirty-Seven Practices of a Bodhisattva* by the master Ngulchu Thogme. After a brilliant summary of the bodhisattva's path, he writes:

> For an inferior intellect like mine it is difficult
> To fathom the vast activity of a bodhisattva,

So I pray that genuine masters will tolerate
All the defects here, the contradictions,
irrationalities, and so forth.

This art of putting oneself down is not limited to literature, but permeates the whole of Tibetan culture, in which humility is an attribute expected not only of realized masters and brilliant scholars, but from everyone, especially those who have accomplished something admirable. Since the opposite is usually the case in our contemporary world, it is important not to take the Karmapa literally when he states, for example, "I don't have much formal meditation experience, so I think it will be very difficult for me to explain meditation today." He followed this put-down with a classic example of his deadpan humor: "Perhaps the organizers knew this and made meditation the topic of this morning's talk in order to test me."

This lowering of himself has the added benefit of making the Karmapa more approachable, less the great lama high up on a golden throne and more the friendly counselor who speaks directly to us and shares his personal experience. In the same way, he makes meditation more accessible. "The main practice I try to maintain is to be mindful and aware in all my activities, whether it is moving about, sitting, lying down, or anything else. I think I do manage to maintain this practice of a moment-to-moment focus in my mind." This, too, recalls another verse from the *Thirty-Seven Practices of a Bodhisattva*:

In brief, wherever we are and whatever we do,
While staying continually mindful and alert

To the state of our mind,
To benefit others is the practice of a bodhisattva.

The Karmapa makes this activity seem simple and easy, but in truth this unwavering attention is the sign of a very advanced practice. If we add in the understanding that since the Karmapa is a highly realized being, he is continually aware of the nature of his mind, what he is actually describing is the state of a buddha.

In a similar way, the Karmapa gives deep teaching in a most casual way. He closed one of his talks by saying, "I do not think this was a fully authentic instruction for meditation, but you could say that I seemed to give a teaching and you appeared to listen to it." After disparaging himself again, the Karmapa demonstrates with a living example how the duality of relative truth manifests as illusion— both subject ("I seemed") and object ("you appeared to") are mere appearance, emptiness inseparable from whatever is arising. Here the Karmapa gave simultaneously the illustrative context and the teaching about it.

For the receptive reader, these jewels can be found throughout the teachings in Canada. To make them more easily accessible, one quote from each teaching has been set at the beginning of its chapter. They are reminders of how the Karmapa has brought forth a profound message in simple and accessible language with an authenticity that connects him with everyone he meets as he opens out the treasures of Buddhism for modern times.

Michele Martin, May 10, 2018

A Note about the Translation

Chapters Two to Five and Seven were originally translated by Tyler Dewar and the remaining six are the work of David Karma Choephel, who reviewed his translations. I listened to recordings of the Karmapa's Tibetan and the translators' English to adjust and edit the translations. The Karmapa's initial greetings to the audience for each talk were similar enough that most were elided though one was left in place as an example, and the conclusions were also shortened on occasion. Except for the words in italics or other speakers who are clearly identified, the entire text is from His Holiness. If there are any errors or infelicities, the responsibility lies with myself alone and I apologize in advance for any mistakes that may have found their way into the text.

Michele Martin

We need to train in loving-kindness and compassion just as we do in physical exercise.

The Karmapa

Chapter One
Love and Compassion Are Critical to Our Lives

First, let us look at a few key points about loving-kindness and compassion as they relate to world peace. Generally everyone wishes for peace and happiness in the world, but when we look at the actual situation here on our planet, we can see that violence has erupted in many places, such as the Middle East. We could lose our hope for world peace, which seems to be slipping off the horizon. But actually, the most important cause for peace and happiness is within our reach — to have peace and happiness in our own minds through the power of love and compassion. This is how we can discover a real hope for world peace, which will be powerful since it is supported by our true feelings of love and compassion. If we doubt that peace is possible or think that there is no need for it, we can counterbalance this by expanding our love and compassion, and seeking peace and happiness within ourselves. To create internal and external peace, taking this path of practice is crucial.

Scientists report and Buddhism teaches that love and

affection are naturally present in all of us. Further, as we are social animals living in community, it is important for us to have love and affection for each other in all stages of life. For example, when parents who are wanting to have children learn of a pregnancy, they think of their unborn child with great affection. It is important for children to be surrounded by this environment of love, for humans cannot live without it.

We are born with the capacities for love and compassion, but they need to be nurtured just like language skills, which are also inherent. If we are not schooled by others and left to grow up in an isolated place devoid of humans, we will not learn to talk. It is the same with love and compassion: we need to be in a setting that allows them to flourish, so it is essential to create a surrounding of affection and love. We can start in our family to instill the value love and compassion. One of the simplest ways to do this is to speak the words "love" and "compassion," connecting them with a child's mind and imprinting a pattern of positive associations.

A couple I know have several children and one of them was temperamental and often angry. The parents were wondering why and then remembered that during the pregnancy, the mother was often angry, and it seems this emotion might have been transferred to the child. Another example comes from my own childhood. My parents often spoke of loving-kindness and compassion, instructing us to respect and love all living beings, no matter how big or small, and not to harm even an insect. This advice and their example created a strong impression on me and my sisters and brothers. Though it may seem like a small beginning, I think such a practice can make a difference in creating harmony among all living beings.

There are many challenges, however, to developing loving-kindness and compassion. Just being content to hear someone talk about them is not enough. We need a sincere and heartfelt enthusiasm to motivate and sustain us, because we will be challenged on this path, mainly by our self-centeredness and pride, which are quite powerful. Our ego fixation causes us to set ourselves apart, thinking that we are special and cut off from others. It is as if we had closed ourselves off in an iron cage of self-absorption. In this state, we loose our consideration for others and only a few people are allowed to connect with us. Slowly the warmth of our affection and compassion for them cools, and they in turn lose their affection and compassion for us. Eventually our relationships will turn cold and we will wind up in a cruel world devoid of warmth and love.

For that reason, we need to train in loving-kindness and compassion just as we do in physical exercise. Fuzzy hopes and tepid aspirations are not enough. We must practice working against our ego's resistance, so that we have the strength to overcome it and become truly loving and compassionate.

Usually, when we say that we are meditating and training ourselves in compassion, we think in terms of a subject and object — an individual subject who meditates on compassion as an object. But we should transcend this duality and come to experience ourselves as embodying compassion and feel that we have become its very essence.

In the final analysis, it is not just an understanding or a feeling of love and compassion that we need. Compassion should be connected with our everyday world and become something we can use and put into practice naturally. What usually happens, however, is that we take how things appear at face value and think of self and other as separate and far apart from each other — I am here and there is someone else out there. But from the ultimate perspective of how things truly are, "self" and "other" are interdependent phenomena that rely on one another. On a deep level, we all are a part of each other.

In Mahayana Buddhism, Avalokiteshvara represents compassion. He has many forms and one of them has a thousand eyes and a thousand arms, symbolizing his engaged compassion — the ability and unwavering dedication to move into action and benefit others in myriad ways. Compassion and love are not some vague hope, fine idea, or pleasant emotion; we must participate in compassionate activity here in this world. When we meditate on compassion, we become able to look at people and the world with the eyes of compassion, so that seeing others itself becomes an activity of love and compassion. In sum we should put our meditation into action and not confine it to some small place where we are sitting.

*The main point about being Buddhist
is that we are trying to become
better people.*

The Karmapa

Chapter Two
Transforming Disturbing Emotions
A Dialogue among the Three Major Traditions
of Buddhism

The broad stage of the Convocation Hall at the University of
Toronto was decorated with brilliant bouquets of flowers, and
three chairs had been set out for the main speakers. His
Holiness the Gyalwang Karmapa, representing the Vajrayana
tradition, was seated in the middle and on his right was the
Venerable Bhante Saranapala of the Theravadin tradition,
who lives at Toronto's West End Buddhist Temple and
Meditation Centre. On the Karmapa's left was the Venerable
Dayi Shi of the Mahayana tradition, who resides at the Cham
Shan Temple also in Toronto. To begin, each master gave a
brief talk, which was followed by a series of questions from the
organizers, and finally, the mike was opened to questions from
the audience.

The Theravadin Tradition
The Venerable Bhante Saranapala

Representing the Theravadin tradition, Bhante Saranapala
was the first speaker. After thanking the other two speakers for

coming, he mentioned that this occasion was the fourth dialogue of its kind to take place in Toronto and that he was glad to be sharing the Buddha's words of wisdom on this important topic of working with disturbing emotions. He began by speaking of suffering.

The early Buddhist teachings understand afflictive emotions as *dukkha* (in Pali). At the beginning of this session today, a film was shown that highlighted the Four Noble Truths: suffering, its cause, cessation, and the path that leads to cessation. *Dukkha* is translated as "suffering," "pain," "disappointment," or "frustration." The word *dukkha* has a very deep meaning and is made up of two words: the prefix *duk*, which means "difficult" and the verb *kha*, which means, "to bear," "handle," or "endure." So *dukkha* means something in our lives that is difficult to deal with or live through.

Now we can ask ourselves, what is so difficult to handle in life physically, mentally, and emotionally? One definition given by the Buddha is a very famous statement from the Pali: "Not getting what you want is very painful and difficult to bear emotionally." There are so many things that are difficult to bear in this life. It could be anxiety, depression, or any other emotional struggles that challenge us.

To deal with our problems, the Buddha taught that we have to follow the model or technique of the Four Noble Truths: (1) we first identify the problem of suffering or what the afflictive emotion is; (2) we diagnose the cause; (3) we know that there is an end to dukkha, that we can stop this problem; and (4) to do so, here is the path we have to follow.

To transform and bring to an end all the emotional problems in our lives, we need to follow the noble Eightfold Path. One of the eight aspects is known as right intention or right thought. The opposite would be wrong intention or wrong thought. The Buddha taught that to end all our emotional struggles, we need to engage in a major paradigm shift. This is also known as selective thinking, and in modern western psychology as shifting attention. We train ourselves to shift our attention from wrong thinking to right thinking.

To give an example, based on the noble Eightfold Path, we can look at three afflictive emotions and the related thoughts associated with (1) lust or greed (craving or desire), (2) anger or hatred, and (3) harm or violence.

We have to shift our attention from negative thoughts to positive ones to counter these three afflictive emotions, so we turn to (1) thoughts associated with renunciation, (2) with love and compassion, and (3) with nonviolence or not harming. When we shift our attention from the negative to the positive, a change takes place within us, both physically and emotionally.

Another step in the Eightfold Path is called right effort, which has four phases: prevention, elimination, cultivation, and preservation or sustenance. What do these four mean? (1) If there is an image that causes negative emotions to arise, we have to train ourselves to stop paying attention to it, and then (2) try to eliminate anything negative that has already arisen in our mind. These first two steps are essential, and afterward (3) we need to train ourselves to cultivate positive emotions, such as love and compassion. Finally (4), we need to sustain these positive emotions, continuing to cultivate them every day in order to sustain our emotional well-being.

These four stages are in line with modern psychological and neuroscientific research, which I find interesting. All our emotional problems come into being because we are focused on things. Buddha said that instead, we should train in looking at how we are reacting to things in our surroundings.

I can give a simple example to illustrate this. We are happy that the Seventeenth Karmapa is here. He is very young and handsome, beautiful to look at. If we just look at him that way, we have to understand, "I am looking at His Holiness the Karmapa with this particular emotion, and I am thinking, "He's handsome, beautiful, so nice." But actually, we should be looking inside. The Buddha said that we should not just look at outer objects, but look into how we are reacting to them. When we do that, all our negative emotions will diminish and our mind will begin to relax.

This process can be applied to any negative emotion. Let us say somebody made us angry. If we just look at that person, we're going to stay angry and upset, but the moment we become aware and realize, "I'm looking at this person with an angry mind," the angry emotion we have will calm down. All negative emotions are the result of being unconscious; when we become conscious, negative emotions will all go away as we transform them into positive ones. So the person you are angry at is standing there in front of you, and you think, "I'm looking at that person with angry eyes. Let me develop love and compassion for them. May I be free from anger and may my enemy also become free from anger." Being a Buddhist helps you to transform your negative emotions into healthy ones.

We do not have much time and I have so much to share with you. The Buddha taught this technique and others for forty-five years, so it's impossible to give his complete teachings in two hours. I have many techniques taught by the Buddha and maybe we can continue this discussion during the dialogue. I wish you the best. May the blessings of the Buddha be with you.

The Chinese Mahayana Tradition
The Venerable Dayi Shi

The Venerable Dayi Shi began by welcoming everyone and introducing his disciple who would translate his talk on how Mahayana Buddhism can transform afflictive emotions.

It is indeed our honor to be sharing with everyone today the three traditions of Buddha's teaching. We must have had a lot of good merit from our past lives because we are not just hearing the name of His Holiness but also meeting him face to face here in this hall today. May we all listen to his teachings from deep within our mind and then take them into our daily lives. Back in the late 1970s, on his tour in Canada, the Sixteenth Karmapa visited us and the Buddhist Association of Canada's Cham Shan Temple and met our founder. It is indeed our pleasure today to meet Karmapa once again as the Seventeenth. Buddhism originated in ancient India and evolved into three major traditions we have today namely, the Vajrayana, Mahayana, and Theravada schools of Buddhism. Although these three traditions varied in language, ritual, and practice, they are simply different expressions of the same teaching of the Buddha. We all share the same core teachings of dependent arising, the law of cause and effect, and recognizing the intrinsic buddha nature in all living beings.

Today, I would like to explore the topic of how to transform our afflictive emotions through the Chinese Chan teachings. In Chan, the First Patriarch was the famous Bodhidharma, who came from India to Nanjing, China, and then settled on Mt. Song. His successor was the Second Patriarch, Huike, who, before he became a monk, was a warrior who had killed many people in battle. After he met Buddhism and took ordination, he deeply regretted his actions to the extent that he could not eat or sleep; he lived in great turmoil with such a distraught mind that he thought he was in hell. So the monk-to-be decided to face Bodhidharma and discuss this with him to put his mind at ease. Their conversation went as follows.

The warrior asked, "My mind has not found peace. Please put it to rest."

Bodhidharma answered, "Show me your mind and I'll put it to rest."

After a long search, the warrior replied, "When I looked, I could not find my mind."

Bodhidharma commented, "Indeed, I have fully put it to rest."

The story demonstrates the Chan tenet that all sources of negative emotions, whether they seem to come from outside or inside, originate from our discriminating mind that clings onto things and craves the illusionary. Once we realize this, all discriminations will cease and our true mind will be revealed. An analogy is that our discriminating mind is like the clouds, whereas our true mind, our true nature, is like the vast sky. The clouds may come and go, arise and cease, but the sky is always present.

The second story I would like to share is about what happened between the (future) Sixth Patriarch Huineng and Master Shenxiu. Their teacher, the Fifth Patriarch Hongren, asked his students to write a poem reflecting the essence of Chan practice. Master Shenxiu came up with this verse:

The body is a Bodhi tree,
The mind, a standing mirror bright.
At all times polish it diligently,
And let no dust alight.

This is indeed a great poem, showing that we use all kinds of methods — meditation, chanting, and so forth — to observe our mind conventionally. This is a wonderful example of this conventional level. However, Master Huineng, who was at an even greater level of practice and prajna or wisdom, replied with another verse:

Fundamentally, there is no Bodhi Tree,
Nor stand of mirror bright.
When there is nothing whatsoever,
Where can dust alight?

The Fifth Patriarch Hongren commented that Shenxiu's verse spoke about conventional truth, whereas Huineng's spoke of the ultimate. His verse shows us that all phenomena in the world, including our discriminating mind and the afflicting emotions, are ever changing and not real in nature. Through a wide variety of practices, we can let go of grasping onto the illusionary and let our true, permanent mind shine through.

We can feel sometimes that we are suffering from illusions and disturbances in our life. A verse from the *Diamond Sutra* states that it is impossible to retain a past thought, seize a future thought, or hold on to a present one. The past is already gone, the future has not yet arrived, and the present thought arises and ceases, arises and ceases, which is why we cannot grasp it. By engaging in meditative practice, we can learn to purify our contaminated mind and live in the present moment. In doing so, our true mind will not be polluted. This is the path to blissfulness and tranquility.

All these teachings I just spoke about were from Shakyamuni Buddha as well as famous exchanges and stories of historical masters. Now I would like to share with you a personal experience in facing suffering and negative emotions. It dates from May 2, 2011, when we hosted an important ceremony for laying the foundation of Wu Tai

Shan Garden in Peterborough. For that day we had invited thousands of guests, but unfortunately, the weather did not cooperate and it rained cats and dogs. Our roadways, even the altar and all the decorations were badly damaged. It was a big, chaotic mess. I am a person of some pride, and during that time, I got quite emotional and disturbed. I almost got angry and screamed at some of my volunteers. My true, calm self and my discriminative mind were battling with each other.

Luckily, I did have some meditative practice, so for a few moments, I calmed myself in this situation in order to settle my negative emotion first. Then I quickly managed not to let the discriminating mind and emotion take over. During that day, I managed to overcome the situation with calmness and to take care of everyone and everything in the best way I could. I am so happy that I practice meditation so I could control my mind and take care.

The Vajrayana Tradition
His Holiness the Gyalwang Karmapa

Here today we are very fortunate to have representatives from three major traditions of Buddhism meeting together to discuss the meaning of the Buddha's teachings. Present with us are representatives from the Indian tradition of Buddhism, from the Chinese tradition of Buddhism, and from the Tibetan lineages of Buddhism. Up to now, I have had many opportunities to participate in various types of gatherings, but I think this is the first time I have participated in a discussion where representatives of all three major Buddhist traditions in the world are present and participating. So this is a great occasion in general, and also for me personally, as I am continually studying Buddhism and interested in learning more about it, so it brings me great delight to be here.

Up to now we've had the good fortune of hearing discourses from these two wonderful monks. Of the three speakers for today's program, I am the youngest one, and that makes me nervous about saying anything at all. Furthermore, I think our time is quite limited this morning, and most of it has elapsed already, so I am triply challenged — I'm nervous to speak, there's not much time, and I feel that I don't really know much from which I could speak. Nevertheless, as I mentioned earlier, I think this gathering gives us a wonderful opportunity and so, in honor of the occasion, even though I may say only a few words, I aspire that they will be meaningful.

We often encounter the terms *Dharma* or *Buddhadharma*, which usually means "the teachings of the Buddha." However, if we look at the Sanskrit word *dharma*, we can find numerous facets of meaning, and the one to highlight here is "transformation." The Sanskrit word *dharma* comes into Tibetan as *chö* (chos), which is cognate with the Tibetan word *bcos*, meaning "to change" or "transform." So here in this context, we could say that the essential meaning of the word *dharma* is "to tame our mindstream" or "to bring about a change for the better within our minds."

In the Tibetan tradition, the great masters of the past

gave direct, potent, and heart-to-heart instructions that arose directly from their own experience of practicing the Dharma. What we can see from the profound instructions they left behind is that they always emphasized that our Dharma practice must be done in a Dharmic way. What does this mean? Different people interpret what it means to practice the Dharma in various ways. Some people think that practicing the Dharma is performing prostrations, making offerings, and engaging in other ritual activities. Others think that it means to study ritual or philosophical texts, and still others consider Dharma to be meditation. Since "practicing the Dharma" is interpreted from various perspectives, I think it is crucial for us to develop a very clear understanding of what the genuine practice of Dharma really is.

Many people come to me and say they are interested in practicing the Dharma, and sometimes they think that this means to change their appearance. For example, someone, who was not doing this before, might be performing prostrations or they might start carrying around a mala and reciting mantras. Others observing this might think, "Oh, they are now practicing the Dharma. They have become Buddhist." People might think this, but actually it would require further analysis to determine whether or not those individuals have really begun to practice the Dharma or not.

To explore this further, I think it would be helpful to share a story from my personal experience. From the time I was born into a Buddhist family and onward, it was easy for me to assume the identity of a Buddhist. Others might have had challenges in coming to consider themselves Buddhists, because they might have been the only one in their family to do so. For me, there were no such difficulties because I was raised in an environment where everyone automatically considered themselves Buddhist.

Then when I was seven years old, I was recognized as the Karmapa. I did not know who the Karmapa was, but I was told I was the Karmapa, so I just pretended that this was the case. I was led off to the monastery and given all kinds of Buddhist studies. So when it comes to the question of being a Buddhist, it was really a choiceless situation for me, and I have always considered myself a Buddhist.

But another question could be asked. I had no doubt that I was a Buddhist, but what if the question were, "Are you a good person?" When I examine myself honestly, I sometimes find that I am a good person, but at other times, maybe not so much. So the answer to this question is rather uncertain when compared to the question of being a Buddhist.

Here, perhaps for many of us, we meet with a very contradictory situation. We have no problem thinking we are Buddhist, but we're not so sure we're a good person. The reality of the matter is that a Buddhist is someone who must have made great advances toward becoming a good person. A true practitioner of the Dharma must be not just an ordinary good person, but an excellent good person. So this thought "I'm a Buddhist" could involve some degree of pretense or self-deception. When we really analyze ourselves, we could find that we are not really a good person all the time. And therefore, thinking always "I'm a Buddhist" is just deceiving ourselves.

Being a Buddhist does not mean that you become a strange looking person who does odd things that other people do not do. It does not entail becoming different in terms of physical appearance or outward behavior. The main point about being Buddhist is that we are trying to become better people. We are trying to become a good person, trying to cultivate a positive attitude and a more spacious heart and mind.

In fact, being a Buddhist involves making changes to the flaws in our personality. This can be very challenging, because some people might react by saying, "Well, this is the way I am and I can't change it. This is just my character." But Buddhism takes a different approach and says, "No, it is your personality, your character, and you definitely need to change it, because it has negative aspects." We can say that we are authentic Buddhists if we can really transform what is negative within us and develop confidence and compassion. Even if we do not want to say we are a Buddhist, a least we have become a good person. So the practice is all about applying remedies to our disturbing emotions and transforming the negative parts of our character. It is important to do this with great strength of heart and decisiveness.

I think I have gone over time and will conclude my

presentation at this point. I am very delighted to be together with you all and especially to be in the presence of these two great masters.

Panel Discussion

The first question from the organizers was about advice in dealing with emotions, such as anger, hate, desire, and stress. How can we deal with them immediately in three to five minutes?

His Holiness the Gyalwang Karmapa

It would be difficult to bring all our disturbing emotions under control in a few minutes, as the Buddhist teachings take a very thorough and detailed approach to dealing with the afflictions. There are Buddhist presentations of the root mental afflictions, the secondary mental afflictions, and so forth, but they can all be condensed into three essential types — desire, aggression, and bewilderment.

Of these three, the destructiveness of aggression or anger is the easiest to recognize and see as negative. Desire is an emotion that we can recognize, but it is more difficult for us to see that it is destructive or disturbing by nature. We might recognize the presence of desire, but not be so sure how negative and destructive it is to have desire operating in our mind. Then there is bewilderment, and since it is bewilderment, we are also bewildered in relation to it. Not only is it difficult to see the flaws of bewilderment, it is also difficult just to recognize its presence in our experience.

Applying remedies for these three afflictions should be

done in stages. We can start by determining which one is the strongest within ourselves. For example, to take the disturbing emotion of aggression or anger, we might find that we are someone who often gets angry and we might wonder what we could do about it. We could use our faculty of retrospective attention (*dran pa,* also translated as "mindfulness") to review our experience from day to day and week to week, asking ourselves: "How many times did I get angry? When did I get angry? What was it like?" In this way, we can study our experience. If we use our moments of anger to learn more about ourselves, then anger will not be something meaningless or some kind of punishment being inflicted upon us, but rather an opportunity to learn about our mind.

By reviewing those times when we got angry, we can come to understand more clearly how anger is a problem for us personally and how destructive it can be. We must use our own personal experience as the basis of our investigation and not merely the explanation of someone else. Using our own personal experience allows our investigation to penetrate our heart.

It is also true that our stronger and more powerful experiences of anger are often the ones that teach us the most: they point out very clearly why and how anger is destructive in nature, what makes it arise, what keeps it alive, and so forth. I'm not encouraging you to intentionally trigger powerful moments of anger, but I have observed that when they do happen, if we apply mindfulness, these outbursts can sometimes be the most instructive to us.

Our master from the Mahayana tradition, the Venerable Dayi Shi, talked about the two aspects of mind, and there are also two minds when we're dealing with destructive emotions. It can feel as if there is one voice in our mind telling us that we should get angry and another voice saying that we should not get angry, and we ourselves are in the middle of these two. We are the ones who must make the decision: Are we going to get angry or not? In the end, we are the ones who must decide how we are going to relate to our own emotions.

But we shouldn't take the whole project too seriously. Sometimes if we get too serious, thinking, "This anger is a huge problem. I must deal with it. It has to go away," this actually invests more energy in the anger itself. When we are defeated by our own anger in this way, it is a more painful and humiliating experience, and therefore, such a heavy-handed reaction is not helpful. Instead of being so grim about trying to overcome our negative emotions, we can allow ourselves to take a playful attitude, "Oh, you want to mess things up for me? Let's see now which one of us is the strongest." If we take that kind of lighter attitude, then even if our anger defeats us from time to time, it's no big deal and not a huge and painful situation. Everything can be an opportunity to learn.

We always should remind and encourage ourselves to relate to our emotions with mindfulness, applying whatever remedies we have found helpful to diminish our negative patterns. If we get into the habit of relating to our emotions with mindfulness for two or three months in a row, applying antidotes will become more automatic; we will not have to force ourselves so much and mindfulness will happen naturally.

Even so, there is a process of getting to know our emotions as they are, recognizing the flaws of our destructive emotions, and then transforming them. This will take three, four, or five years, and maybe even more. So knowing the benefit, it's important that we continue and not lose heart or allow ourselves to become discouraged.

The next question was for Venerable Bhante Saranapala about his personal experience in training policemen and firefighters.

Venerable Bhante Saranapala

Before I respond to the question about training firemen and first responders, I would like to relate a personal experience in handling disturbing emotions. I tell many stories to my friends, colleagues, and students, and one of these happened in 2000 when I was studying for my Masters degree at McMaster. I was staying nearby the university and one day as I was going to class, I noticed someone who was looking at me with an angry face. I did not pay attention to him, but followed one of the techniques taught by the Buddha: When you notice someone who is angry and upset, do not pay attention to them. However, as I was passing by this person, he yelled at me, "What the hell are you doing here?"

I stopped and looked at him and said, "Sir, I am a student at McMaster University."

He asked, "What's that thing you're wearing?"

25

To him I looked like a complete alien in these robes, so I answered, "I'm a Buddhist monk and this is my uniform. I don't have much time and do not want to be late. Let me go to the campus. I know that you are angry and upset. May you be well, happy, and peaceful.'"

"What did you say? he asked, and I repeated it. He said, "Wait a minute! Can I have a few seconds with you? I want to talk to you. Can I have your phone number?"

Now this is a stranger who yelled at me, and I was thinking, "Here is a real test. I am a simple Buddhist monk. I have nothing to gain and nothing to lose." So I said "Ok. Here's my number." But I never thought he would call me. That evening he did.

"Can I come and see you?" he said. Here's a person who has yelled at me, who is angry and wants to come and see me. What if he kills me or does something else violent? Then again, I am a Buddhist monk and this is a real test to see if love and compassion work, I said, "Yes, you can come."

The next day he came, so I opened the door and offered him a seat. I said, "Sir, I'm a student and don't have much. I have juice, cookies, and some donuts. Please help yourself." He was so surprised and then he sat down. He had come to argue with me, and at the same time, I was treating him with kindness, so he completely changed and became very interested in my story. I told him about my whole life and showed him some pictures.

He couldn't believe that he was talking to a Buddhist monk. We talked for three hours, and after that we became good friends. "Sir, if I invite you to my wedding, would you come and bless me?" he asked. I said, "No problem, just let me know when and where." So I went to the wedding, and they had an official program. When it was my turn to come on the stage to bless them, my new friend took the mike and told the audience, "This is the damn Buddhist monk who changed my life."

So this is my personal story, which I tell to everyone. If you are getting angry and upset with other people, you are not being a Buddhist. Transforming anger to loving-kindness and compassion shows a real Buddhist character and attitude. It is the real technique: I don't have to look at the angry person but at myself. "Ah. I'm looking at this person with an angry mind. This person is reacting to me with anger, and I have to chose to react to them, not with anger but with love and compassion." It works and this is the best remedy.

The last question from the organizers was about mindfulness and meditation as alternatives to drug-based therapies for people with mental issues. What advice would you give someone about this? Should they rely on doctors and science or the Buddhist teachings?

His Holiness the Gyalwang Karmapa

I think it would be good to look at this question from the point of view of the individuals who come to discuss their problems with me. It is true that most people do not come to see me when things are going well for them, but when they are experiencing difficulties and hardships. Of course, some people come who are happy and that's fine as well, but for the most part, they are going through various types of difficulties, which include both psychological and physical problems.

In some cases, I'm not sure if I can help them or not, but I always try to do whatever I can with a motivation that comes from the depth of my heart. Some of their problems can be ameliorated by the advice I might have to give or the light I can shine on their situation from my perspective. But with regard to the more serious psychological challenges or psychiatric issues, I really feel that these individuals would be better served by mental health professionals. These situations are beyond my ability to help, and they also include times when the brain itself is damaged. In these cases, people should definitely consult a doctor.

Another comment I would make is that particularly in our cities, many people struggle at times with mental issues and especially stress, as their minds are not at ease. For some of these people, I think meditation and mindfulness can be beneficial by encouraging them not to take their problems quite so seriously. So in some situations, these techniques can be really beneficial.

Questions from the Audience

How do we balance what is right for us with advice from teachers we respect? How do I decide what I am supposed to do?

Venerable Bhante Saranapala

Thank you for asking such a beautiful and pragmatic question. I know there is so much to digest as we have talked about so many techniques and presented a lot of different information. The Buddha's teaching is not just about believing. You could say that His Holiness is my hero, my master, and therefore, whatever he says I should do. Or Venerable Master Dayi Shi is my hero, and I respect him, so what he says I should do. Or I love Theravada Buddhist monks, and therefore, whatever they say I should follow. However, this is not Buddha's teaching.

There was a famous sutra (in Pali, *sutta*) called the *Kalama Sutra*, which is a story about the Kalama people in the Buddha's time. The Kalamas' village was located near an entrance to the forest, and there were various individuals going into the forest to meditate. When a master came out of the forest, the very first people he met were the Kalama people. The master told them, "Kalamas, I have been practicing meditation in the forest for many years. I know the truth. I have discovered the remedy, the solution for our problems. Therefore, whatever I say is the truth and what the others say is not." Then this master would go away and another master would come out of the forest, denigrate the previous master, and praise his own teaching, and so on it went, one master after the other.

During that time, the Buddha came to this village. The Kalama people thought, "He is such an enlightened master. He will know the truth," and so they went to see him. The Kalama people said, "Venerable Sir, we are confused. Masters are coming out of the forest and each one of them is praising their own teachings and denigrating that of others. We do not know who is telling the truth."

The Buddha replied, "Kalamas, it is good that you are

confused. Don't just believe anything. You have to test the teaching." The Buddha then set some conditions for belief: One should not believe something because of one's parents or teacher, or because it sounds good or logical, or because it has been practiced in a lineage for a long time. These are inadequate reasons. The Buddha advised that when the Kalamas heard a teaching, they should test it in practice. Through their experience, they would know if it would be good and beneficial for them, for some others or everyone. If it passed these tests, then they should feel free to follow that path.

My question is about the larger good. In our contemporary world, is it possible not just for the sangha but for nations as well to look for the larger good, beyond the self-interest of the industrial age? Can we hope that this might happen?

His Holiness the Gyalwang Karmapa

Yes, we can have hope. Dialogues are already happening between various communities and individuals. And it is not just spiritual traditions discussing this topic among themselves, but scientists are getting together with representatives of spiritual traditions, and they are expressing their desire to assume a collective responsibility for the welfare of the world. I think that this interdisciplinary and intercommunity dialogue should be continued and expanded so that spiritual traditions can converse more with each other and with scientists. Beyond this they can set up exchanges among these communities and representatives of social workers and of people in many other fields.

Coming together and sharing our ideas and inspirations will definitely increase the collective goodwill that exists in the world. We can definitely hope for this.

We are shifting from old habits that are narrow, inaccurate, and stiff into new ones that are vast, precise, and open.

The Karmapa

Chapter Three
Ground, Path, and Fruition
Session I

After greeting everyone and expressing his delight in the cultural diversity of Toronto in which Tibetans have flourished, the Karmapa turned to the subject of his talk. He explained that he was asked to speak about the specifically Buddhist topic of ground, path, and fruition, which is a vast category that, in fact, encompasses the entire Buddhist journey with all of its practices and teachings. Since it is such an immense topic, he noted, it might be challenging for him to speak eloquently about it in a short time, but he would try.

The first of this triad of ground, path, and fruition is the ground, which basically means the actual state of things, or we could say, the true nature of phenomena, the way things truly abide. "Ground" refers to the basic condition or the actual status of all phenomena, so the teachings about the ground introduce us to this profound reality.

The true nature of things is something that is present within us and does not change regardless of whether we realize this nature or not. Nevertheless, if we fail to see reality as it is, we will encounter numerous difficulties and hardships. For us to see this nature, we have to practice developing a correct viewpoint or an authentic way of looking at things. In working on this, we can come to the point of seeing true reality as it is.

When presenting the view, Buddhist philosophy often discusses the principles of emptiness and no self, because these two are considered key for developing the correct view. But in terms of the true nature of reality, view is all about developing a way of looking at the world and maintaining a perspective that allows us to see without error what is going on.

If we were to speak about the reality of no self in a very simple way, we could take a look at how we usually conceive of ourselves with the thought of "I" and "me." What is it that we think we are identifying when we have that thought "I" or "me"? What does the mind that thinks that thought actually look at or believe? If we investigate, we will come to see that our assumption of an "I" or "me" comes from thinking that our "self" is an independent entity that does not depend on anything else for its existence.

But if we look more deeply into that assumption, we can discover that actually, we are not independent individuals — our existence relies on many other people and things. In fact we are very dependent, and this "I" or "me" that we think we have, cannot stand all alone on its own ground. There is no phenomenon to which we can point and identify as an independent entity.

When we think of ourselves as an "I," one of the first reference points that comes to mind is our body. In other words, we usually look at our body as the basis for the thought of ourselves. Our body, however, arose in dependence on our parents, and its continued existence depends on other things, such as the food we need for nourishment and the clothing we need for warmth. So our body, the very basis for our thinking we are independent, is itself just the opposite — completely dependent.

There can be some misunderstanding about this profound dimension of reality due to the impressive and powerful sounding words *selflessness* or *no self*. Some people hear these words and think that they mean there is no self whatsoever, that there is no such entity at all. But this is not quite the meaning of selflessness. Instead of erasing the self, the teachings on emptiness encourage us to explore what our self really is — to look into the way in which the self exists or does not.

One of our most fundamental habits is assuming that we are self-sufficient and separate. But the teachings on selflessness point out the basic reality of the self as continuously dependent on others: we live in a world of mutual dependence, interconnectedness, and dependent arising that links us to a vast array of people and things.

Some people might wonder about the meaning of selflessness and have doubts, so it is important to find a clear understanding. Selflessness should not be understood as a full stop, a period that terminates all discussion. Instead, we should consider selflessness as being more like a question mark. When they contemplate selflessness, however, some people relate to it as if it were a final decision that had already been made for them. They say, "Well, there is no self and that's that." But this is not really the correct way to approach the study and contemplation of selflessness. What we need is an attitude of inquisitiveness that leads us to explore further.

If the Buddha taught that the self in some way does not exist, we need to learn what he meant by that. In what specific way does the self not exist? What is the distinct way that the self operates in terms of true reality? We could approach these questions with a sense of delight and curiosity. Selflessness is not a commandment given by the Buddha that we must follow; rather, it is a teaching by the Buddha that we are meant to explore for ourselves, based on our personal experience, so that we can develop our own clear understanding of it. If we can blend our direct experience with the teachings of the Buddha on selflessness, then we will be able to develop an understanding that is truly profound.

As I mentioned before, the Buddha did not say that the self is utterly nonexistent, but rather that our self does not exist in the way we assume it does. We can start off by examining our usual conception of the self, looking further to see if there is a truly existent self that matches our assumptions and thoughts. This process of exploration should not be separated from our day-to-day experience, but intimately connected to it. We can look at our daily lives and see how we are dependent on others to stay alive.

All of the food and clothing we need to sustain ourselves comes from others. If we reflect like this in an ongoing way, we will develop an authentic experiential understanding.

Some people could approach their studies and contemplation of selflessness and emptiness as if these were a series of fixed statements to repeat after the Buddha. But actually, the Buddha cannot replace us when it comes to investigating what our reality is. It is up to us to do our own exploration and analysis, and then decide for ourselves. In this way the teachings on selflessness will have brought us some actual benefit.

Sometimes, people who come to see me say that they do not have much wisdom or clear seeing intelligence (*sherab* in Tibetan or *prajna* in Sanskrit). Some people say to me, "I don't have much wisdom. Please give me a blessing so that I can develop it more." Or they say, "Please open the gateway to my wisdom." But prajna is not like that. It is not something I can open up for people right away or transfer to them by some means.

There are many explanations and classifications of prajna. Succinctly, we can say that it is the wisdom realizing the true nature of reality. Prajna is enhanced while we are training in the view. To expand our wisdom, we need to develop an unmistaken view of what the true nature of things is. This involves deep personal reflection and changing the habits of the way we think and understand, so we can move from a narrow way of seeing into one that is broad and vast. We are shifting from old habits that are narrow, inaccurate, and stiff into new ones that are vast, precise, and open.

The main focus at this first stage of the ground is to develop the clear wisdom that sees things in a vast way, embracing the entire panorama of reality. Obviously, this kind of wisdom is not something that can simply be given to someone: it has to develop within each individual. We must work with our habits — the way we usually see, think, and understand — and shift from being narrow and biased into being open and objective. This is how we come to see clearly things as they are.

Therefore, training in the view is not just about learning the tenets of various philosophical systems, though it does involve studying them. The main purpose, as just explained, is to make our perspective vast and our minds open and clear. Some people have taken a mistaken approach to training in view, and instead of their minds becoming more spacious, they contract around a specific philosophical interpretation. The result is that their study has the opposite of its intended effect and their mind narrows down instead of opening up.

Thus there is no guarantee that engaging in philosophical studies will lead to a clearer, more open mind. If we do not engage in studies properly, they can lead to a narrow outlook. The main point is that we should approach view with an open-mindedness, a willingness to investigate a position, not from one but all sides, and a willingness to reflect upon the reason for any given conclusion. It is important to keep this in mind when we study Buddhist philosophy.

Related closely to *selflessness* is another key term *emptiness*, which is central to Buddhist view. In Sanskrit the word for emptiness is *shunyata* and its main part *shunya* means "zero." What are we doing when we study the view of emptiness? We are letting go of our old assumptions and long-standing habits that we have cultivated mentally. By using our mind to reflect on emptiness, we clear away this thick covering of thoughts and bring our mind back to its original starting point, its basic ground, so we can start from zero and see the world freshly. This process allows new wisdom to take birth within us and provides a space in which a deeper knowing can arise. Emptiness has this very special capacity.

In sum, the approach we take at the initial stage of the ground is to develop a relationship with reality as it is. This points to the essential meaning of what His Holiness the Dalai Lama intends when he talks about a science of mind. The emphasis is on finding out the reasons for any given position or habit through investing the facts of our direct experience with our own intelligence. From this perspective, the process of training in the view is not actually religious per se: it is not about taking on a religious way of being, not about adopting customs or following prescribed rituals. Rather, we are seeking the reasons for why we hold onto a particular belief or why we maintain a certain attitude. We continually practice to develop our wisdom, and in this way we come to a deep confidence in our own relationship with reality.

I think this is a good point to conclude this first morning session and we will reconvene in the afternoon.

"Traveling the path" means that we gain
increasingly profound experience
of our true nature.

The Karmapa

Chapter Four
Ground, Path, and Fruition
Session II

This morning we began the exploration of a famous triad in Buddhist teachings, known as ground, path, and fruition. We began our discussion by exploring the meaning of the term *ground* and how it points to the basic nature of things, the actual situation of reality. In turning to this, we could start to relate to reality by using our ability to reflect as a support for our view of the world and for how we approach life.

We discussed how developing a correct view of reality is not just the special domain of scholars or philosophers, but directly applicable to our present lives, and even more than before, critical to how we move through this twenty-first century. When it comes to topics, such as the value of human life and the ideas related to it, it is important to develop a coherent view based on reason, so that we have a firm understanding of the intrinsic value of human life. Using our intelligence, we can also consider how to develop our ability to cherish and value our lives.

The second component of ground, path, and fruition is the path. As traditionally presented in Buddhism, the most fundamental element of the path is known as the Three Jewels, the Buddha, Dharma, and Sangha. When we enter the gateway of the Dharma, it is taught that we rely on the Three Jewels as the basic support for our path of practice — they are the root and heart of all the Buddha's teachings.

Of the Three Jewels, the Buddha is the one who shows us the path, the guide who knows how to traverse it and who can teach us how. The Dharma is the path we travel to liberation. The Sangha are our companions on the path, those who accompany us and ensure that we move correctly along it.

The Dharma is central to the path since our destination is the state of liberation or omniscient buddhahood, and the path leading to it is the Dharma. In general, there are many different paths that lie before us and numerous choices we could make about which one to go down. Some of the paths are familiar, and we know many other people who have followed them. Other paths are not so familiar, and we are not connected with many people who have traveled on them. In the end we usually choose the most familiar path, as it feels more convenient and safer; we know more about it and the people who have chosen it. The path we do not know seems scary and dangerous so we have our doubts and turn away.

Yet it is also true that precisely this lack of familiarity could make the path less traveled seem attractive to us. We could feel curious about this unknown path. What might happen? For the very reason that the path is new and unexplored, we have a sense of delight and a greater interest in knowing what it might be. At the same time, since it is less traveled, there are fewer people we can consult. In the context of Dharma, it is the teachers or spiritual friends to whom we turn, because they are familiar with this extraordinary journey we want to take.

Originally, it was the Buddha Shakyamuni who took the path of practice and traveled down it to the final destination of full awakening, so the Buddha is considered the most authoritative guide for those on this path. The Buddha, however, lived over 2,500 years ago, so even though the Buddha's teachings and the Buddha himself are reliable guides for the path, his life has become more like a story or a legend, so we need to rely on a more recent source of knowledge that is trustworthy. We look for a living person who has traversed some of the path and can give us the details we need to know. Such a spiritual friend can encourage us and, especially when times are tough, they can remind us of the path's benefits and its ultimate goal.

Yet, even if we rely on a living spiritual friend, at the end of the day, we have a long spiritual journey to make all by ourselves, and arriving at our destination is not going to be easy. This is why the teachings state that we as individuals must develop a sense of trust and confidence in what we are doing and where we are going. Learning to turn inward is the essential point of meditation.

It is true that our own experience is not hidden from us; nevertheless, since we do not see ourselves clearly, sometimes it is easier for us to have confidence in others rather than ourselves. When practicing the Dharma, however, we will have difficulties if we lack self-confidence and a true belief in ourselves. Anchored in the Dharma, our mind should be decisive and stable in its confidence. If not, our practice will not bear fruit. It is also true that even though we need to trust in ourselves, sometimes it is difficult to locate our self-confidence. When we practice the Dharma, we spend a lot of time searching for the truth within, seeking to find out exactly who we really are. This is learning how to be more confident in ourselves and in our insights, and also enriching ourselves with genuine positive qualities. We spend a lot of time in these endeavors when we practice the Dharma.

Once we discover that this practice of looking into ourselves is actually the main practice of Dharma, we can see that the notion of path and destination is simply an analogy: there is not an actual place, some literal destination called liberation, that we come to. The true picture is simpler: we are becoming more familiar with ourselves. "Traveling the path" means that we gain increasingly profound experience of our true nature. As we see this abiding nature more clearly, we are truly traversing the path — this is how we actually arrive at the destination called liberation. Understanding this, we know that liberation is not some place outside of us, and the path to it is simply a process of seeing more deeply.

Actually, if we think about it, the analogy of the path as something stretching from a beginning to an end is not really an accurate image. Instead of this linear process, a truer analogy would be moving from the outer to the inner, from the circumference to the middle point. First we start on the outer level and then practice brings us closer and closer in, until we arrive at the center and see our own true nature.

Generally, this process is thwarted by our usual way of thinking. We always want things to be better than they are in the present moment. We have the habit of feeling that the way things are now are a bit too plain, too simple, too ordinary. We want our situation to change so that our experience is more amazing and impressive. To a certain degree, we all have this habit of thinking. We go astray when we bring this habit of thinking into our Dharma practice and approach the Dharma as a consumer or materialist. We want something superior and wonderful, something high and very special. If we receive these impressions, we feel we have really received a good teaching. But if there is an opportunity to receive teachings that we consider more common or run-of-the-mill, we think that they are not worth much.

Some students of the Dharma might rely on a lama for refuge and bodhisattva vows and later on regard that level of teachings as too low, so they look for another teacher who is more famous or willing to give teachings the student considers more profound. They leave their original teacher behind, and when others ask them, is not such and such a teacher yours? They answer, "Oh, it's just someone from whom I received refuge and bodhisattva vows." They look down upon the teachers they consider inferior in some way and fail to realize the great value of what they have received.

The main point is that feeling appreciation is really important. Appreciation can help us to develop many other positive qualities and connect us with a profound experience of well-being. For example, in meditation, the breath is often used as an object to focus our minds, and we can learn a great lesson from our breath. When we are alive, breath happens all the time as a basic function of our body. From this perspective, breathing is no big deal — it is something that our body does all by itself. We do not have to pay attention for breathing to happen; we can be breathing and not particularly aware that we are.

In the practice of meditative concentration, however, we adopt the breath as a special object on which we intentionally focus, placing our attention on every single breath and becoming intimately and continually aware of our breathing as it moves in and out. When we do this, certain insights naturally arise in our mind. We come to appreciate that breathing relies on certain causes and conditions to make it possible. If it were to stop, our lives would cease as well. The moment we recognize this, we develop an appreciation for our breath, seeing it as simple and ordinary, yet critical to our continued existence. When we have this insight, even though breathing is so simple, we can see how beautiful and amazing it is, and naturally, we are filled with a feeling of great appreciation.

When we foster this attitude, our idea about happiness

might change. We might realize that in order to be happy, we do not absolutely need a particular type of car or house. It might occur to us that just this ordinary breath, in and of itself, is filled with well-being and happiness, and this is enough. That is just one example of how we could approach the path. In terms of a formal presentation, I will leave it at that for the time being.

Transforming Disturbing Emotions

Yesterday I participated in a conference on transforming disturbing emotions and I think it would be good to pick up the thread of that discussion. As I mentioned before, the path of Dharma is about developing a relationship with ourselves and exploring the question of how to relate in a skillful way with our own mind and experience. When we honestly examine ourselves, we may find that our greatest challenge is within — our own painful and disturbing emotions.

That is why all of the Dharma that the Buddha taught focuses on methods to tame our disturbing emotions. It is said that there is no Dharma teaching of the Buddha that was not given for the purpose of working with our mental afflictions. We could say that all the teachings of the Buddha are ways to tame our mind stream and deal with our emotions. The perspective that I usually emphasize is to turn our attention inward to face ourselves and our own emotional landscape rather than turning our attention outward and escaping into distraction.

It is easy for us to focus outside and comment on the

emotional problems of others, describing their flaws and confusion. But when we direct our attention inward to ourselves, suddenly it is not so easy to talk about where the problems are. Why? When it comes to our own afflictions, we look outside for someone or something to blame and say, "That situation is the reason why I feel this way. That person or that group of people are the ones who caused my problem and made me have this feeling." This is our habitual way of deflecting our gaze from what is actually happening, but the truth of the matter is that our emotions come from within us. If we are experiencing emotional difficulties and upheavals, we are their source. This is a more accurate description of how things are, but it is difficult for us to accept.

In many countries today, there is an emphasis on freedom of speech and thought, which we hold to be very important and rightly so. It can be a bit strange, however, to look at the ways we use these freedoms. To a great degree, we are free to speak our minds to people high and low about the faults we see. However, we should remember that we are also free to look at ourselves and see what our own flaws and confusion might be. While free to look at the problems of others, we should not forget that we can examine our own emotional problems and afflictions. I think we should take advantage of this freedom as well.

One of the slogans from the teachings on mind training states, "Drive all blames into one." "One" here refers to the collection of negative emotions we harbor within. This slogan encourages us not to find excuses on the outside, to which we can assign the blame for our afflictions, but instead, to turn and look inside for the source of our troubles. When we do this, our real research has begun; in the Dharma, our search for truth starts like this.

If we can turn our attention inward to focus on our own confusion and come to recognize our disturbing emotions, we have begun to accurately locate the sources of our suffering and difficulties. Clearly identifying these basic causes starts the process of freedom from suffering. If we avoid this process and keep our attention focused outside while continuing to blame others for our afflictions, it will be hard to get at the root of our problem. The end result would be an unhappy world of people continually casting blame on each other — actually, not too different from the way things are now.

As I mentioned during the "Dialogue on Transforming Disturbing Emotions," of the three poisons, anger is the easiest to see; desire we can see but do not always consider negative; and ignorance (or bewilderment) by its very nature is difficult to ascertain. Since we cannot identify ignorance in our minds, we do not recognize it as problematic and a source of problems. Buddhist texts often speak of ignorance, so we can study it extensively, but in terms of our own experience, it is difficult to pinpoint it and say, "This is the affliction of ignorance."

It is somewhat like this with all of the disturbing emotions: we gain some understanding when various aspects of the afflictions are explained, but until we directly identify them in our own experience, we cannot begin the necessary process of working to change them. Mere intellectual understanding does not move our heart to the point of making a real shift. As long as our knowledge of the disturbing emotions remains in our brain as intellectual information, it will not really move our heart so that change can happen. We should fully commit to studying ourselves, so that our heart is deeply affected and change can actually take place. This is the only way transformation will happen on the path of practice.

The main point of meditation is learning how to relax the mind within itself.

The Karmapa

Chapter Five
Finding Freedom through Meditation

The topic of this morning's talk is meditation. Ideally, if you were going to have someone explain meditation, you would want that person to have a certain amount of meditative experience. But in my case, I really do not have any special experience of meditation practice. Journalists are always asking me, "What is the first thing you do when you wake up each morning?" I think they ask this as a leading question because they have the expectation that I will answer, "The first thing I do when I wake up is meditate," since this is the answer His Holiness the Dalai Lama has given many times.

Actually I feel somewhat embarrassed when journalists ask me this question. I cannot say I do not do any practice, because I do engage in some contemplation, mindfulness practice, and so forth. But at the same time it is difficult to really say that I am genuinely doing the practice of meditation in a formal way. The main practice I try to maintain is to be mindful and aware in all my activities, whether I am moving about, sitting, lying down, or doing anything else. I think I do manage to maintain this practice of a moment-to-moment focus in my mind. Apart from that, I don't have much formal meditation experience, so I think it will be very difficult for me to explain meditation today. Perhaps the organizers knew this and made meditation the topic of this morning's talk in order to test me.

As all of you know, throughout the world these days, there is a growing interest in the topic of meditation and mindfulness. Statistics from Google give evidence of this new attraction. What they show are high numbers for searches on topics linked to meditation, but if we look at the statistics for the term *Buddhism*, the numbers drop off sharply. This tells us that many more people are searching for information about meditation than want to know about Buddhism. I think this is because Buddhism has been given the label "religion," which has a negative effect on people's interest. Meditation and mindfulness are not burdened with this label, so people connect with them more freely.

From one perspective, the situation is good news, which we should welcome and pay attention to. It is wonderful that more people are curious about meditation, and we should support this trend. From another perspective, there are elements of this movement that are a bit worrisome. What I see in some cases is a tendency to use meditation for commercial purposes. This is concerning because it would be a great loss if meditation were separated from its original values and the rich traditions in which it grew.

The practice of yoga has gone through phases. Originally in India, yogic practice was strictly spiritual: it was a closely held secret and its practitioners were immersed in spiritual pursuits. In our contemporary world, however, yoga can often be commercialized for secular purposes. The concern is that something similar could happen with meditation.

Actually, the practice of meditation is very personal. Turning it into a business would rob meditation of its broader and deeper context (of philosophy, social engagement, and ethics, for example), which we should appreciate and sustain. Valuing this wider dimension allows us to stay connected with the authentic sources of meditation. With this in mind, I feel it is very important that before meditating, we examine our motivation for engaging in practice. We need to take a close look at our purpose for meditating. What is our goal? Why are we doing it? Analyzing like this, we should try to develop as much clarity as possible, so we know what we are doing and why.

In looking at our motivation, we create a clearer and more transparent environment in our mind, and this influences the quality of our mediation and how it evolves. Sometimes we become so focused on the techniques of meditation that we lose the bigger picture — what kind of mental landscape we are creating for ourselves. We can also spend a lot of time worrying about whether or not we are correctly practicing a particular technique. But if we look carefully at the situation, the mental atmosphere we create — in other words, the basic attitude we bring to meditation — is more important than how accurately we perform some method of practice.

To illustrate this, we can look at a story from the biography of the Third Karmapa, Rangjung Dorje (1284-1339), who was famous as a great meditation master, and many of his students were reputed to have been accomplished meditators. One day someone approached the Karmapa and asked, "I've heard that there is a spiritual instruction that allows you to achieve liberation without practicing meditation. If such a thing exists, please give it to me."

Rangjung Dorje replied, "Yes, such an instruction on nonmeditation exists, but if I were to give it to you, I am not sure it would help you, because I am not certain you would be able to understand and realize it. You might practice some contrived meditation rather than the true intent of the instruction. So even if I were to give it to you, I do not think this teaching would help you." When it comes down to it, meditation techniques are not that important. The main point of meditation is learning how to relax the mind within itself. Learning how to simply let go is the essential point of meditation.

In the practice of shamatha, or calm-abiding meditation, the main instruction is to allow our mind to rest one-pointedly on an object of focus. We concentrate the energy of our mind and direct it in a focused way. An analogy for this is pouring water through a pipe. These days in our modern world, and especially in busy cities, people's minds are constantly distracted to all the outer objects in the stimulating world of urban life — the constant display of material things and mundane concerns steal away our attention.

To counteract this, the practice of calm abiding encourages us to draw our mind inward, rather than letting it be pulled outside. We learn to let our thinking mind be settled and at ease in a state of peace. In sum, we do need to bring a certain effort into the practice of one-pointedly focusing our mind, but we do so in a relaxed way. This one-pointed focus, as well as being relaxed, is very important for the practice of meditation in general.

Meditation usually involves an object of focus, which helps our mind become more settled and our attention more directed. The object can be external, like placing a physical object before our eyes and directing our complete attention to it, or the object can be an internal image created by our imagination, to which we direct our focused attention. Working with these different objects are all methods for settling our mind.

The practice of calm abiding can also happen in relation to our breathing. Used as a focal object, the breath has special advantages. For example, since it is always present with us, we do not have to search for it somewhere else, but just direct our attention toward it. Relating to the breath gives a simple and convenient reference point for meditation.

To meditate in this way, we focus our attention one-pointedly on the breath, involving our minds 100 percent; you could also say that we have full appreciation of our breathing or that we taste our breath completely. We then abide in the continuum of this practice, placing our attention on the breath and trying to be as fully attentive to it as we can without any interruption, appreciating one breath after another. If we cannot focus like this continually, there is no need to worry and we can just relax. It is important to be at ease while focusing on the breath. Some people think that they have to make relaxation happen intentionally, but this is not really what is meant here. Rather, the real meaning of relaxing is not to make an effort, because if we do, then, of course, we are not relaxed.

In the manuals for meditating on Mahamudra (*chagya chenpo*, the Great Seal) and on Mahasandhi (*Dzogchen*, the Great Perfection), we read instructions that encourage us to rest our mind directly within the movement of the mind or directly within the thinking mind or directly within the perceiving mind. Instructions such as these are teaching us how to relax in meditation. It can happen that if we are unable to focus in the beginning on the object we have established as our reference point, we worry and wrestle with our mind to get it focused again.

However, the Mahamudra and Mahasandhi traditions instruct that if we cannot focus on our point of reference, we can simply rest our mind in that very state of not being able to focus. If we find that we can focus, then we rest our mind in that very state of being able to focus. What we do not do is worry when we cannot focus initially. There is no need to panic when we discover that our mind has slipped away. If we can be relaxed within our mind, even when different objects appear, we will be able to remain in a state of mindfulness, and our basic awareness and attentiveness will continue uninterrupted.

Another misunderstanding that we might have is treating our mind as if it were a heavy object, which we are squarely placing on our breath to anchor it, but this is not a beneficial approach. Some people have told me that when they practice this meditation on the breath, it stops, and since this is very uncomfortable, they have to quit. It seems that they are taking too solid an approach and treating mind as if it were a heavy object that presses down on the breath.

That kind of practice will not help us. Rather, we should experience our mind as something fluid like flowing air that is moving together with the breath. When we are breathing out and air is moving through our nostrils, we simply think, "Ah, the breath is going out," and we let our mind flow together with the breath. So the quality of our attention should be pliable — not tense but free of fixation and stiffness. We can let the mind be as light as air flowing gently along with the breath. In contrast, some people treat the mind in meditation as if it were a sniper staring through the sight of a gun, tight on the target. This constriction is not what we are looking for in meditation; rather, our minds should be light and fluid.

Furthermore, when we meditate, we breathe naturally as we usually do. There is no need to make a special effort and force our breath into a special pattern — we just breathe normally. Also, many meditate by counting the breaths, numbering the rounds of breathing or how many inhalations or exhalations they have. I think that for the time being, it would be better not to emphasize counting the breath and simply relax while keeping a gentle focus on the breath itself. This is because counting the breath in addition to maintaining a focus can make the practice a bit too complicated and busy. For now, it is better to relax and not count.

To set up periods of meditation, the common instruction states, "Do short sessions many times." This is a good practice to adopt; however, the situation is not so simple if we really want to practice in a very complete way and accomplish the qualities of calm abiding as explained in the traditional texts. These qualities cannot be achieved merely through a light or casual relation to meditation. Properly speaking, calm abiding and its qualities are achieved through months of intensive practice in retreat.

If we do devote ourselves to months of shamatha and really delve into it, we can come to embody the qualities of a mind that abides in a state of peace. Apart from that, just doing a little bit of practice on a daily basis will not take us that far. Of course, it has the benefits of helping to calm our mind and increasing our ability to focus, but it will not bring us all the way to the state of calm abiding as taught in the traditional texts. Furthermore, these days, even doing retreat is challenging. The texts say we should go to a secluded, remote place but now cell phone connections reach even isolated areas.

Another key point is to do the meditation correctly from the very beginning of our practice. If we can put our energy into practicing properly from the start, there is a good chance that our meditation will progress well. But if we start out with bad habits, they will set up tendencies that will eventually interfere with our practice, and it will be difficult to remove them at a later time. One of the most challenging things about meditation is that it can be quite boring; it is not exciting in the way that we usually like to be entertained. Actually, our mind is like a child, needing excitement and constant distractions. A child can focus for a short time, but then runs off quickly to something else.

We should be aware of this tendency and head it off by setting a clear intention to be patient and persevere through those stages that might be uneventful or boring. Sustaining our meditation in this way allows it to progress. However, if at the start, we fall into bad habits and give into our distractions and cravings, it will be hard to eliminate these negative habits later on, and they will inhibit our practice. Instead of dragging ourselves to the cushion, we could feel excited about our meditation; rather than wanting to be entertained and thrilled by something else, we can develop a full-hearted enthusiasm and delight for the practice.

Let us turn briefly to the process of perception as it relates to meditation. In general, we are immersed in the five sense consciousnesses, which relate to the perception of forms, sounds, smells, tastes, and objects of touch. Our mind is continually distracted by these five sensory objects and immersed in the pleasures they provide. However, meditation is centered on the sixth, mental consciousness, and the pleasure we enjoy in meditation is that of meditative focus (*samten, bsam gtan*). These days there is a great emphasis on external development, and this outer world is mainly connected to these five sense consciousness. Our society does not give us a lot of support for relating to the sixth consciousness and the pleasures of meditation. Our contemporary world is a challenging environment to live in from the point of view of meditation.

It might help here to give an example. Where I grew up was quite remote and had little modern development. Though we had some comfort and ease, it was nothing like the quantity and variety that are available today. In one way, you could say we were poor, yet in another sense, you could say that our life style, the way we related to the environment, and our notion of enjoyment was very similar to the indigenous peoples of North America.

We did have things to enjoy, but not in the same way that things are available today in such vast abundance and astonishing variety. Instead, we basically enjoyed the same types of things that our ancestors had enjoyed for hundreds of years. There were not many new things and it was certainly not like today with products coming out all the time to generate more excitement and entice us with further entertainment. Whatever our parents and grandparents wore, that was what we wore. Whatever food they ate, that was what we ate.

It's difficult to say that the comfort we knew was the same as the pleasure of meditative concentration, but perhaps it was not too far off. Our minds were very content and we did not have many worries. By contrast, if we look at our contemporary world with its impressive advances in so many fields, it seems that misery has kept pace with all the developments. The more industrial and technological advances we have, to that extent, we see increased suffering and lack of contentment.

I think we can conclude here. This was the best explanation of the practice of meditation I can offer. I do not think this was a fully authentic instruction for meditation, but you could say that I seemed to give a teaching and you appeared to listen to it.

At a deeper level, we are all part of each other.

The Karmapa

Chapter Six
Compassion Is More Than a Feeling

Our situation in this world is such that we are always in mutual relationships with each other. Especially in this information era of the twenty-first century, it is clear that thanks to technology we are interconnected more than ever before. And yet, when we consider relationships, we usually do so in a way that distorts them by thinking in terms of "self" and "other." This "self" is on our side of things and that "other" is on the far side over there; we identify the two as different and separate people who are not related. But actually, we are all interrelated. And at a deeper level, we are all part of each other. We all participate in the experience of pleasure and pain, and we share responsibility for each other as well.

Actually, compassion is not such a heavy burden for us to carry. The very nature of responsibility is courage or strength of mind. Responsibility means that we develop our confidence and hope as well as awaken our capacity for kindness and compassion. Seeing responsibility in this way, we can take it on willingly and enthusiastically.

Scientists as well as Buddhists explain that the capacity for loving-kindness is innate or hard-wired; it comes with us into this world. Depending on a child's surroundings, this innate ability either expands or shrinks, so it is important that our environment increases our capacity for love and compassion and also encourages us to be supportive of one another. Unfortunately, in today's world it is easier to find situations that promote violence rather than nurture compassion. It is not that we lack loving-kindness, but we need an atmosphere that will foster it, so we should encourage and support each other in this.

It is in our families that we begin to develop these positive qualities. They can provide a world supportive of peace and loving-kindness though their actions and also simply through using often the words *kindness* and *compassion*. This can make a real difference. When I was young I lived with my parents, who were not educated but had inherited a tradition that emphasized kindness, and not just for people, but for all living beings whether large or small. We were taught to always respect and protect animals down to the smallest insect. This teaching placed a positive imprint in our minds, reminding us not to harm living beings or be violent. When we grow older, we have to face numerous problems and difficulties, but at least when we are young, we can receive the gift of positive thoughts. Over time these imprints can deepen and become stronger.

When we think of loving-kindness and compassion, we

often think of compassion as sympathy, perhaps empathy, or sometimes as understanding someone else. Like this, we are actually dividing our experience in half: the subject who has the compassion and the object for whom compassion is felt. Normally, we feel that these two are separate and think, "I am meditating on compassion for that other person." But in fact, we should feel that the person for whom we feel compassion is actually a part of ourselves and that our hearts and minds are fully involved with them. Compassion is not just an understanding, but also the feeling of our hearts and minds being completely involved with another person. Through practice, we eventually come to embody compassion and are able to convey it so clearly that the other person actually feels it.

When we meditate on compassion, if we sense that we who are feeling it and the object of our compassion are separate, then we still need to develop our compassion. Only when we who are meditating on compassion truly become it, have we truly developed the power of our compassion to the extent that we can feel that others are a part of ourselves. This is real compassion.

At this point, compassion is not just a feeling, but turns into an activity that we do; it becomes an instrument for our way of helping in the world. Through meditating on compassion, we come to actually feel compassion looking through our eyes. And due to our motivation, when we are listening, our hearing is imbued with compassion. Likewise, when perception through all of our five sense faculties is suffused with compassion, it is not just a feeling, but turns into an activity and a tool for benefitting others. Once we have engaged in the stages of meditation on compassion, for example, when we are talking with people, our presence is filled with compassion; our experience is not divided into self and other, and gentle words come naturally. We should make a great effort to become like this.

Everyone is looking very serious now, and from one point of view, perhaps this is a serious thing; however, from another, maybe it is not so serious since we all have an innate capacity for compassion. Yet due to the surroundings in which we live, it can be difficult to develop and manifest it.

When we are young, it is important to develop compassion for all forms of life. As I mentioned earlier, I grew up in a nomad family, so sometimes we had no choice but to kill animals. When we had to do this, I had a deep feeling of love and compassion. I do not know if it was the authentic compassion described in all the texts, but it was an uncontrived, naturally arising feeling. Since then, I have experienced no greater feeling of compassion. Nothing compares. Over the years, I have studied many texts, but the compassion coming from all this effort is merely contrived. It is not better than the natural feeling of compassion that I felt as a child. This is a feeling that we all have had and need to cherish.

Limited natural resources cannot fill our unlimited desires.

The Karmapa

Chapter Seven
Mindfulness and Environmental Responsibility

It is a great pleasure to have this opportunity to be together with all of you at the University of Toronto. I offer my warm-hearted greetings to the professors, researchers, students, and to all who have gathered here. I am delighted to be in Canada for the first time and to visit in this beautiful city. Toronto has such richness and diversity thanks to the many peoples of different backgrounds, who have come to make their lives here. Through respecting and valuing each other's cultures and religious traditions, they are able to live together harmoniously. All of this makes Toronto a special place.

Tibetans are one group who have come here, and actually, their number in Toronto is greater than anywhere else in North America. Not only do they have the opportunity to preserve their unique spiritual tradition and culture, but they are also a part of a multifaceted array of people living amicably together, so they have the opportunity to share their traditions with others and learn from them as well.

For these many reasons, I first want to express my gratitude to this city and all of its inhabitants.

In this complex world of ours, numerous differences can appear based on religion, politics, or ethnicity, and these separations are created through our ignorance. If we take the perspective of the natural environment, there are no such divisions between us; from nature's point of view, we all spend our lives together on this single planet. In its vast matrix of life, we exist in a profound relationship of mutual dependence — our own happiness and suffering depend upon these connections with others. In this realm of interconnectedness we spend our lives.

If we could take a real interest in the environment, it would allow us to see that basically, we are like one living being, as we are all sustained by the very same planet. And no matter how many relationships, positive or negative, we might have with each other, by focusing on the environment, there is a good chance that our understanding will become broader and clearer.

Today's topic is connected to the environment and I would first like to share with you my personal experience. I was born into a nomad family in a remote area of Tibet, and we followed the same customs that nomads had followed for centuries. From the time I was born until the age of seven, I had the wonderful opportunity to inhabit and experience this world.

Thanks to these years lived in the direct experience of nature, I have an appreciation for nature's beauty, the wish to protect it, and a sense of what helps or harms an ecosystem. These days, if we take a look at the people who live in cities, few would have had the chance to experience such a world. When I was living with my family, we knew nothing about environmentalism or how such issues are defined and discussed. However, having lived in such a deep way as a child, I have a spontaneous interest in the natural world and working to benefit it in some small way.

Nowadays, the question of the environment involves everyone on the planet. It is also the greatest challenge we face in this twenty-first century. Scientists are doing research and monitoring the environment while also creating relevant technological tools, which are greatly needed. However, it is not only the research and the tools that are important to develop; we must also develop a clear philosophy of science and articulate an ethics of what is beneficial and what is harmful. This philosophy and ethics should be correlated with whatever scientific knowledge we gain.

But scientific knowledge in itself is not enough to change people's minds and motivate them to act. Knowledge is important, but knowledge alone tends to stay in our brain and not change our behavior in a practical way nor does it spur people to take on personal responsibility for the environment. We should use our tools and knowledge not just as methods to gain and retain information, but to move into the next step of altering our behavior and transforming our sense of responsibility.

For this to happen, it is not only scientific knowledge that is useful; we can also draw upon various forms of traditional knowledge and customs. There are wise and wonderful stories handed down through the generations that preserve sensitive ways of relating to the environment. There are also numerous teachings and practices preserved in the various spiritual traditions of the world that can instruct us how to relate to the environment in a positive way. All these resources can aid us in transforming our motivation and in becoming more mindful. If we can combine scientific discipline, cultural traditions, and spiritual wisdom, and if the representatives of these different fields can come together and pool their efforts, I think there would be great hope for changes in the environment and our well-being.

These days, it seems that everyone is taking an interest in the topic of mindfulness. Many people, however, relate to mindfulness as isolated individuals or they might use it to shield themselves psychologically, so in fact, they are really just taking an interest in themselves alone. But the practice is not merely a question of "my mindfulness," for it is not only about oneself. We should consider mindfulness in the much broader context of looking at the richness of the profound, mutual relationships between ourselves and others and between ourselves and the environment.

As I mentioned before, there is a lot to talk about in relation to the environment — the science, accumulated knowledge, textual traditions, ethics, and so forth. In the end, though, it comes down to the vital point of each person making individual choices and decisions. If this does not happen, all the science, textual traditions, or stores of knowledge we have remain mere information. It is up to us to engage what we know and examine it, thus bringing our intelligence to life. Therefore, it is important for each of us who are practicing mindfulness to reflect on how we are harming or helping the environment.

Likewise, in conjunction with whatever environmental study we do, mindfulness is key for training and developing our understanding. Since each and every one of us influences the environment, all of us together must work to sustain a positive relationship with our natural world. It is not just the scientists who are experts in the environment who should take this responsibility; all of us must carry it in partnership with each other.

If we were to ask, "What is the main reason for environmental problems?" At the top of the list would be our cravings to acquire and consume. Our desires are insatiable, and we set no limit to them, forgetting that the natural resources we enjoy have a cut off point. Limited natural resources cannot fill our unlimited desires. In whatever way we can, we must reduce and restrict our craving for more.

Question and Answer

How do we maintain mindfulness when confronted with hostility or a problematic situation?

It's not enough merely to say the word *mindfulness*. We have to really engage in the practice, applying it in a pragmatic way to our day-to-day lives. Sometimes we become very busy running around here and there doing all kinds of things. At the end of the day, if we look back to see what we have done, we cannot pick out even one thing we had accomplished to our satisfaction. Sometimes we cannot even remember what we did. But mindfulness is about being present to our actions and being aware of what we are doing while we are engaged in it. Mindfulness makes our relationship to daily life more clear and brings a greater appreciation of our lives.

Another aspect of mindfulness practice is relating to our afflictions and bringing them under control. A big part of mindfulness is not letting our mind follow whatever habitual patterns it likes, but watching it very carefully and looking at our thoughts and emotions attentively. We can try out this practice and see what happens. I think it is important to approach mindfulness with a sense of playfulness, perhaps a bit like a game or an experiment. We can look to see what effect mindfulness practice has on our experience. Have we developed more clarity and understanding in our day-to-day lives?

Thinking or reading about mindfulness does not suffice. We need to actually engage in the practice and give it a try. It's not enough to hope it could help or to say "Oh, that sounds like a good thing to do." We have to really engage and see for ourselves what happens. And we can be a bit playful about it as well.

How can people step away from fear-based thinking?

There are different types and levels of fear, so it's difficult to give one all-encompassing answer to your question. In relation to the variety of fears, there is a variety of remedies. For example, when we are young, we can experience fears without knowing the reason why. Sometimes these fears arise due to old habitual tendencies in our mind.

In my own experience of working with fear, I found that if we can turn inward and find an internal sense of support within ourselves — a strength or positive energy that can serve as a reference point to which we can turn — this will help to reduce fear. When we have trouble connecting with a basic sense of well-being, it is easier to slide into a state that feels vacuous or unsupported if we do not connect with this inner resource.

Sometimes it is not yet possible to face the fear directly and begin dealing with it, so instead of focusing on what we are trying to overcome, we could focus on what we are trying to accomplish and develop this within ourselves. In this way we work with fear not by focusing on it, but in turning to what is positive within us. This can lead to a different feeling as we gradually reduce our fear. As I mentioned in the beginning, however, it is difficult to give a blanket response to this question.

Given the resistance to climate change from some leaders, what can we do to influence the current situation and create a positive result?

I think many of us share a feeling of concern and discomfort, even shock, about the current state of things. In considering the global environment, we are looking at a vast and complex world, so sometimes it is difficult to see the immediate effect of our actions on this situation. In terms of the environment at this scale, the effects of our actions can seem quite limited, and seeing our powerlessness can be discouraging. A useful approach is to keep our minds open, letting our awareness be panoramic. Within this wide space, we act locally, relating to our neighbors, our friends at the office, and to people we meet in these smaller contexts. At this level, we will be able to see some effect from our actions. I am sure you all have heard, "Think globally, act locally."

Our brain sems to be wired so that it responds to immediate stimuli and dangers. For example, if a tiger were to leap right in front of us, our flight mechanism would be triggered and we would react immediately. However, if someone said, "In two months a tiger will come along and jump at you," we would certainly not react in the same way. Our relationship to environmental issues can be similar. We have the knowledge that things are getting serious, but we lack the impetus to translate that information into an immediate action. It is absolutely crucial that we do not deny the reality of the problems in the environment, that we do not procrastinate until it becomes too late to do something about them.

What do you foresee for the future of the earth? Is it possible for people to change? Can they become less greedy and more concerned about taking care of the environment?

To start by using myself as an example, as I mentioned before, I lived as a nomad for the first years of my life and meat is a staple of our diet. Perhaps 80 percent of our meals have meat in them and vegetarian fare makes up most of the rest, though people are trying to increase this traditional vegetarian side of their diet. In my case you could say that not only did I like meat, I loved it. Later, after I came to India, I began to change my way of thinking, seeing the suffering eating meat caused and the many ways it is harmful to the environment. In thinking about meat from different angles, I gradually began to feel differently to the point that now when I see meat, I feel rather uncomfortable. This is an example of a change that really took place.

Sometimes these changes need time, but we should be careful not to use time as an excuse not to change. At some point, we need to make a decision, and that takes courage. It is not that we lack courage, we have it within us, but it needs to be activated by conditions. When we meet with the right circumstances, they can make our courage powerful enough that we are inspired to change. Inspiration can come from within ourselves or from outer conditions, such as coming to a deeper appreciation of the environment, seeing the condition of animals, or witnessing the excellent conduct or activity of another person. Whatever it might be, we need inspiration to help us shift our habits into becoming really passionate and decisive about changing. Considering this potential for transformation, I think there is truly hope for the world.

The challenge here is that people want their comfort and fear any discomfort. Change feels threatening because we are so accustomed to our old habits, which are easy to follow and feel right. We hesitate to shift anything because discarding what is ingrained and taking up something new involves some hardship. What we need, therefore, is more courage, and I think there is hope that we will find it.

It is essential that we do not think of Avalokiteshvara as the object of our meditation, but rather as the subject that is none other than ourselves.

The Karmapa

Chapter Eight
Compassion Does Not Stop at Empathy
Excerpts from an Avalokiteshvara Initiation

Before bestowing the empowerment, the Karmapa remarked that most people at the event would know that Avalokiteshvara embodies the loving-kindness and compassion of all the buddhas. He takes the form of a bodhisattva, but in actuality he is a buddha. The Karmapa's teachings below are excerpted from the explanations he gave as he bestowed the empowerment.

The empowerment today is for the mantra, or the dharani of Avalokiteshvara. There are many names you could give it, and today we are emphasizing the practice of his Six-Syllable Mantra and receiving the permission in the form of an initiation to practice it. Mantras have been called the "declaration of truth" or "words of truth," which is how the word *mantra* is sometimes translated into Chinese. The reason for this is found in sutras belonging to the foundational vehicle. They state that even at the time of the Buddha, there were such declarations of truth and relate the story of Angulimala after he had gone forth (left home) and became ordained.

One day Angulimala was going on his alms round and he saw a woman having great difficulty and pain in giving birth. He was unable to do anything to help her, so with great concern, he returned to the Buddha and described the woman's suffering. The Buddha instructed Angulimala to go back and say to her, "Since the time I have gone forth, I have never killed anyone." Before becoming a monk, Angulimala had killed many people, but since that time, he had refrained from killing. After making his statement, the Buddha counseled that Angulimala should make the aspiration: "If these words are not mistaken, by the power of their truth, may she give birth easily." Angulimala returned to the woman and followed the Buddha's instructions. Through his declaration of truth, she was able to give birth easily. This story illustrates that a declaration of truth is telling something as it is — it is not false, but honest and authentic.

The Six-Syllable Mantra of Avalokiteshvara, OM MANI PADME HUM, is equivalent to his name. How is it then that his name becomes a declaration of truth? From the time that he first aroused bodhicitta and became a bodhisattva until the present, he has always acted in accordance with his promise of bringing benefit and happiness to all living beings. Due to this stable, unchanging commitment, Avalokiteshvara's name has become a mantra — a declaration of truth that manifests the unwavering and lasting nature of his promise.

The reason it is important for us to meditate upon ourselves as the body of Avalokiteshvara is that it gives us the opportunity to stop thinking of ourselves as ordinary beings. Seeing ourselves as Avalokiteshvara brings us encouragement and eagerness to practice and help others. Further, when we are meditating upon ourselves as Avalokiteshvara — the embodiment of the compassion of all the Buddhas — getting angry is more difficult and also a little embarrassing. So when we have the pride of being Avalokiteshvara, we feel differently than we did before and have greater confidence.

It is important to know that initially Avalokiteshvara was an ordinary being just like us. When the great compassion of bodhichitta unfolded within, he was transformed into Avalokiteshvara. We are no different, because the same capacity to develop compassion and loving-kindness for others is naturally present within us from the time we are born. If we can expand that capacity, we will become like Avalokiteshvara. Since this is possible, it is important that we have the courage and confidence to take this path.

Avalokiteshvara, therefore, is not just a sacred being, worthy of veneration, prostrations, and offerings; he is also an example of what we can turn into, of how we can follow the path and come to embody compassion as he did. If this were not true, it would be difficult to say we have the same capacity as Avalokiteshvara. So it is essential that we do not think of him as the object of our meditation, but rather as the subject that is none other than ourselves. This motivation and perspective guide our practice: we visualize ourselves as Avalokiteshvara so that we will become compassionate just like him.

For the next initiation of the mind of Avalokiteshvara, we rest in equipoise, inseparable from his mind, which is nondual wisdom. This is possible because the essence of all sentient beings is buddha nature. From this perspective, Avalokiteshvara and all beings are the same: there is no distinction of one being better and the other worse. It is not as if the mind of Avalokiteshvara is one thing and our buddha nature is another; rather, it is like pouring water into water. Now we should rest in equipoise, meditating on the meaning of this nature and remembering how the dharma expanse, the nature of all things, actually is. Resting this way is the initiation of the mind.

Actually, just reciting the mantra is not enough. The mantra we recite orally and what we think in our minds should be in harmony; otherwise, our meditation is just pretense. Looked at from the outside, it may seem as if we are practicing the Dharma, but in reality we are not, so there is no point in practicing this way. What we recite orally and what we think mentally should match.

The compassion we talk about in Buddhism is not merely the sympathy, empathy, or pity that we usually feel.

The compassion taught in the Dharma is a stronger compassion than the normal one; it is more involved and more dedicated, because we do not see ourselves as the ones who have compassion and the individual for whom we have compassion as separate. It is not as if the person who has compassion is in a good position and the other person is desperate, so we are having pity on them. Rather, the other person becomes a part of us. Through practice, we become the nature of compassion, so we are able to give ourselves over to it and fully dedicate ourselves. This allows us to take responsibility for compassionate activity in the world and mentally bear the burden of it. In sum, this compassion is not merely a feeling, an idea, or an understanding. It is not merely a prayer or wish, "May it be so" or "May this person be better off." What is crucial is that we actually put our compassion into practice and integrate it into what we do in our lives.

Sometimes people have doubts about the form of Avalokiteshvara. They wonder, "Well, he has four arms, so how can his shoulders work?" They wonder even more about Avalokiteshvara with a thousand arms and a thousand eyes. Actually, this is not so important. The main point is that whether he appears with four arms or a thousand arms, his form indicates that in actual practice, he is more involved and more dedicated. Having many arms means that a single set is not enough. This multiplicity symbolizes that Avalokiteshvara has an immense number of connections with living beings and a vast dedication to benefiting them.

Sometimes I have the feeling that just one single person is not enough to benefit all living beings. I am not Avalokiteshvara, of course, but I try to do as much as I can for others. I can feel that just one single person is not enough to do this work. As one person with only two arms, what can I do? It seems to me that I need to be able to create in front of every single being, an emanation that can do what would help them and what they wish. Only then will I be able to bring benefit to them. Otherwise, as an ordinary individual with only two arms, it is difficult to actually help everyone.

When Milarepa gave rise to compassion, he said, "Developing compassion feels like being thrust into a huge pit of fire." The feeling of true compassion is as intense as being engulfed by fire. It is as unbearable and overwhelming as being burnt alive and that is how it should feel. Sometimes, when we think we have compassion for other people, we just say, "Oh, the poor thing! So sad." and leave it at that. There is no power or impetus to this at all, so it does not benefit because we are not moved to do anything. Our compassion should come from deep within and, expanding from there to include all beings, it brings us to create a positive effect in the world around us.

*Freedom is not a question of
external conditions but of
mastery over our mind.*

The Karmapa

Chapter Nine
Interconnectedness
Our Environment and Social (In)equality
The Gyalwang Karmapa and
Professor Wade Davis in Dialogue

Professor Davis

First of all, it is a tremendous honor for us to have His Holiness with us and an honor for me to be on stage, as so many of my colleagues could have easily been in this place. It is a great gift to me. We in Canada are fortunate to have received teachings from so many remarkable Tibetan spiritual leaders, including the visit here of His Holiness the Fourteenth Dalai Lama. Sometimes we can forget how special these moments are. Some years ago, I traveled 4,000 kilometers across Tibet with a friend, and when we reached Lhasa, we went to visit his mother. She spun the wall of her home to reveal a hidden devotional chamber, for which she could have been imprisoned if discovered. I rather thoughtlessly and causally mentioned that I had met His Holiness the Dalai Lama. Instantly she began to weep and took my forehead to hers. I can still taste the salt of her tears. In that moment I understood what it meant for Tibetans to be in the presence of His Holiness the Dalai Lama or His Holiness the Karmapa. So this is something that we as Canadians should be extraordinarily appreciative of.

The word *Karmapa* means "the one who performs the activities of the Buddha." These activities do not have to be exclusively religious in nature. This extraordinary book, *Interconnected*, the latest one by His Holiness the Karmapa, is less about Dharma per se than is it about all the key challenges of our age, examined through the filter of the Buddhist way of thinking. As the Karmapa writes, "The aim of the book is to calm our minds, and think more clearly and carefully about the direction in which we are going." Of course, the point of Buddhism is not to convert people, but to contribute to their well-being.

It is said that Buddhists think of themselves as being ill, see the Buddha as a doctor, the teachings as the treatment, and spiritual practice as the process of being cured. Following this, I have structured my questions to His Holiness to address initially the challenges alluded to in the book, while the later questions will address the solutions, his essential intuitions, and insights that provide all of us a path forward, a roadmap of hope.

One of the important themes of the book is that we are not only interdependent, we are in every way interconnected — in both our inner and outer worlds — for better or for worse. At one point in the book, the Karmapa stated, and I paraphrase, that the water you drink is the same as that which slaked the thirst of the dinosaurs. The air you exhale allows plants to eat light. He also mentions that when Jackie Kennedy took a liking to leopard skin pillbox hats and matching coats, within a few months, a quarter of a million cats had been slaughtered to satisfy a fashion fetish. The cheap shirt you are wearing may have been made by a young girl in Bangladesh, who was lured to the city to escape grinding poverty and work for a pittance just to survive. Everything is interconnected.

The first question I'd like to ask His Holiness is a question he poses in the book itself: How would things change if we began to actually feel our interconnectedness? What human values would come to the fore when we acknowledge our interdependence emotionally, psychologically, and spiritually? What would a global society that fully embraced our interconnectedness really look like? What can we do to create such a society?

The Karmapa

Interconnectedness simply means that in the reality of how things are, everyone is connected one to the other. We live in a socially constructed reality, however, and these imprints shape our attitudes and how we see things in ways that lead us far away from how things actually are. To see interconnectedness, we first have to find a different viewpoint, another way of seeing our actions and the things around us. Rather than settling into our old ways, we need to find new perspectives.

In our usual mindset, our sense of being a self leads us to think in terms of "us" and "them." However, we should take an interest in this duality and deeply question the idea of an independent self that does not rely on anything else.

99

It is only when we investigate the self that we can begin to understand interconnectedness.

Professor Davis

That touches on a fundamental Buddhist notion that the feeling of being apart from everything in the universe is just an illusion and the idea of an "I" or "me" is just a concept. The Buddha said that the self does not ultimately exist and he illustrated that with an example from the realm of desire. He noted that our perceptions of an object as being desirable or not, does not reside in the object itself, but in the way we perceive it. There is a wonderful Buddhist saying that illustrates this: To her lover, a beautiful woman is a delight, to an ascetic, a distraction, and to a wolf, a good meal.

A sense of separation is something that the book addresses as it looks through a Buddhist perspective at the challenges we face. For example, His Holiness notes that thanks to the Internet, we are more connected technically than ever before, yet this connectivity leaves us feeling emotionally disconnected and isolated. Part of this is that when we engage through the Internet, we actually think we are engaging with a human being, be it on Facebook or YouTube, but we are actually engaged with pixels and nothing more.

It is also true that the Internet could emerge as a kind of global campfire. As we navigate that world, however, we have to maintain the realization that it is by definition illusory in nature. We see pixels on a screen and hear a digital reproduction of a person's voice, yet when you get down to it, there is nothing there. So we feel puzzled when our virtual connections actually leave us feeling disconnected and drained. What is missing, His Holiness writes, is the fullness of human contact.

It gets even worse, he suggests, as our constant connectivity can end up trivializing our lives. He notes that in families today, members send text messages from one room to another or even while siting at the same table. We begin to live virtual instead of actual lives.

The Karmapa

In one way, information technology does bring us closer, because we can clearly see what is happening in other parts of the world. But actually the Net is just a tool that we are using; it is not an actual connection. A real connection is a feeling, an emotional relationship between people. We have a friend we can meet and talk with; we can hold their hand or give them a hug. The Internet is just a device, not an actual relationship. Being clear about this difference is one of the greatest challenges of our times.

Professor Davis

Another important theme in the book is a very strong stand on the environment. I am fascinated by how His Holiness's childhood influenced his attitudes toward the environment. We're only beginning to get spiritual leaders, yourself as well as Pope Francis, for example, coming out strongly on environmental issues, climate change, and water. You write in the book, "There is absolutely no basis for thinking that the earth's water belongs to some people more than others. Our thirst is felt equally and our bodies depend equally on clean drinking water. The water we have belongs to all species on the planet."

You also write about growing up as a nomad in Tibet and what leading a life completely divorced from modern technology meant to you. Is that the source of your commitment to the environment?

The Karmapa

I think so. Until I was seven, I lived in nature. Afterward things changed when I became the Karmapa. Before then, I had the opportunity to lead a very traditional nomadic life that was close to nature, for which we had a strong respect. It is also true there was little modern development. We were eating the same food and wearing the same clothes as hundreds of thousands of our ancestors did. That made me appreciate the traditional way of life and also the connection with nature.

Professor Davis

When you were very young, you were recognized as the reincarnation of the Sixteenth Gyalwang Karmapa, and at the age of eight, you were giving teachings in front of 20,000 people. In 2000, you had to leave Tibet to go to India, and yet you carried with you the spirit and feeling of the Tibetan environment into your adult life.

The Karmapa

Yes, when I was young, I lived close to the land. Before I

came to India at the age of fourteen, I did not have the chance to reflect on the environment, as I was busy with other things. After coming to India, however, I had the opportunity to think about the environment and realized that when I was in Tibet, we did not have the concept of protecting it. What we did have, however, was a natural respect for the environment, based on customs that were passed down through many generations. Only when I came to India did I discover that respecting the environment had a special name and that there was a need to protect it. In India, I began to learn about the larger world and I think that improved the way I think.

Professor Davis

Another theme that runs through the book is something the Buddha spoke about over 2000 years ago and to this day we do not acknowledge it even though we have been warned time and time again by all the wisdom heroes of every culture and civilization: To seek happiness through worldly pursuits can never bring true inner peace. It is as hopeless, the Buddha once observed, as casting a fishnet in a dry riverbed.

And there's a very powerful line in your book: "Greed is a hunger that only intensifies the more we feed it." I would be delighted if His Holiness would comment on that line.

The Karmapa

When we look at the environment in general, we face many different crises, such as global warming, which are huge issues, so huge actually that we do not know where to start. But if we really think about these difficulties, we can see that they come down to individuals and their greed, which is the cause of our problems. The environmental disasters we face are due to the destructive effect humans have had on the natural world — these are related to our greed.

Most of us cannot distinguish between our wants and our needs, so we confuse one for the other, which creates serious problems. This confusion is abetted by commercialism, which invades our lives through television, newspapers, and the Internet. We are surrounded by media, which continually stimulates our desires and leads us to think that we need everything that is advertised. If we do not have these things, we are some kind of failure. The problem is that our wants have no limits, whereas our natural resources do. If we continue in this way, scientists say that even if we had the resources of five or six earths, this would not suffice to fulfill all our desires. So the most important point, the real key, is that we have to limit and control our desires.

Professor Davis

Reading this book, you would almost think the Karmapa was an anthropologist. When we reflect on something like global warming, which has become society's problem, it was not created by humanity as a whole, but by a subset of humanity with a particular mechanistic view of the world — our lineage going back to Descartes. Many of the communities and cultures that are suffering the direct impact of climate change had nothing to do with its creation. Ironically, they are the ones trying to do more in their cultures to mitigate the effects of climate change through ritual and other activities than we are in the West, and we are the origin of the problem.

You write very beautifully about the gifts that other cultures give us. The fundamental lesson of anthropology is that every culture has something to say, each one has the right to be heard, just as none has a monopoly on the route to the divine. You write, "We must listen attentively to other traditions, taking care not to project our own meanings and assumptions about what they are telling us. If we do so, as we engage with new ideas and new practices, ultimately, they will change us and allow us to discover new possibilities for living as humans on this planet."

And that, of course, is the whole gift of cultural diversity — the realization that other peoples of the world are not failed attempts at being us. Every culture is a unique answer to a fundamental question: What does it mean to be human and alive? And when the people of the world reply to this question, they speak in 7,000 languages. Of these 7,000, we know that half are not being taught to children. Friends among the Musqueams, our local First Nation people, are struggling to preserve their language, as are the Tibetans. What is it that we need to do to address this question of language loss and waning of cultures? How to support the rights of all people to have their voices heard?

The Karmapa

We could approach this question from another perspective. When people think of Tibet, many do so in terms of politics. However, if we reflect on the world's supply of water, for example, after the North and South Poles, Tibet has the largest reserve of fresh water stored in glaciers and snow. What happens in Tibet affects not just Tibet, but the entire continent of Asia, so this is a very important issue.

Actually, in order to protect the Tibetan environment, we have to protect the Tibetan culture and language because they are intimately connected with the natural world of Tibet. The Tibetans have lived on their land for thousands of years and have a profound understanding of their environment. The way they interact with their surroundings reflects a wisdom gathered over a long span of time, and it is critical that we safeguard it. So when we talk of preserving culture and language, it is also important to realize that we are preserving the experience and wisdom about the environment.

Professor Davis

I'd like to move this toward the positive. There's a great line in the book in the discussion of compassion, where His Holiness says, "Apathy kills more than any single disease." What did His Holiness mean by that?

The Karmapa

Both Buddhist beliefs and scientific presentations state that human beings are born with a capacity for empathy.

Due to the way we train our minds, however, it can be switched on or off. The primary reason for saying, "Apathy kills more people than any single disease," is that when we look at the world, we see so many people who are impoverished, who do not have enough to eat, sufficient clothes to wear, or a stable place to call home. War is a cause of further suffering and painful difficulties. We can see these situations with empathy, but we lack an affection powerful enough to move us into helping other people in a concrete way.

If we clearly look at the world, we can see that there is no reason for people to suffer so terribly. Yet, due to apathy, we do not take action. Even if we do feel a strong connection, it is for those near to us; we do not care for people outside a boundary we have created. We need to extend the limits of this confine to include as many people as possible. Our aim should be to expand our embrace of others and make it as vast and inclusive as possible.

In Buddhism, we talk about giving rise to bodhichitta — the wish to benefit all beings and bring them to liberation — which means stretching our hearts and minds to encompass increasing numbers of people. If we could do this, the apathy in our world would diminish and there would be no need for so many people to be living in misery. This is the relationship between apathy and all kinds of suffering, including disease.

Professor Davis

On the topic of empathy, His Holiness has a wonderful,

concrete solution. Apparently, there are scientific methods available that can measure empathy neurologically. He writes, "I have a proposal. Before a country holds political elections, candidates should be required to undergo neurological studies to determine their level of empathy. Just hook them up to the machines and see how they do. If they fail the test, they should be required to undergo training until they come up to a certain mark, and only then be allowed to proceed with their election campaigns. This may seem absurd, but imagine the impact it would have on the quality of life on this planet if we were to take empathy seriously as a qualification needed in order to be given the opportunity to lead the world."

There is also an insightful discussion in the book about the nature of freedom. Less in Canada, but certainly in the United States, freedom is taken as a license to do what you want. The basic motto of American civilization is "Don't mess with me," which is why when Mahatma Gandhi was asked what he thought of American civilization, he said, "I think it would be a good idea." Oscar Wilde commented, "America is the only place where you can go from birth to decadence without passing through civilization."

There is a beautiful passage in the book about authentic freedom. His Holiness states: "Freedom does not mean doing whatever you want in the moment. The Tibetan term for freedom actually translates as 'self-control' or 'self-mastery.' Being in control of oneself is happiness; being controlled by what is other is suffering. An authentic freedom needs to include freedom from destructive emotional forces. Authentic freedom is rooted in wisdom as well as understanding and respect for interdependence. Freedom begins in our hearts and minds but it must reach its fruition in the broadest possible context of universal freedom from suffering. Authentic happiness is complete freedom from any reason to suffer.

The Karmapa

Speaking from my personal experience, when I was seven years old, I was identified as the Karmapa. I did not seek this out nor did my parents. A group of people arrived, with whom we had no connection, and said, "You're the Karmapa," and that was it. People have often asked me, "Were you happy to be the Karmapa or not? You were just seven and did not have the freedoms that other children had." Honestly speaking, it would be difficult to say that I was happy. But then again, it would be difficult to say I was not. Being the Karmapa is a great honor and good fortune, but I cannot really say whether it makes me happy or not.

In my sense of things, there's a big difference between being happy and leading a meaningful life. Happiness is a passing emotion, whereas being meaningful may not have much emotional coloring, but deep down it brings contentment.

People talk about different kinds of freedom, and in the physical world, it is difficult to find complete freedom. To discover true freedom, we have to look inward. This kind of freedom does not depend on others, but on how we are dealing with our selves and our emotions; we are able to live in a more harmonious way with both of them. Freedom is not a question of external conditions but of mastery over our mind.

Professor Davis

There's a wonderful line in the book which explains how we can continue through life, keeping our shoulder moving the wheel in a positive direction: "Generosity of spirit helps to keep our aspirations limitless even when the results of our efforts are limited."

We have an obligation to bear witness to the world, which reminds me of the First Noble Truth that all life is suffering. The Buddha did not mean to negate life, but to state that terrible things do happen. Evil is not exceptional but a part of the existing order of things, a consequence of karma. I think that you can realize that your actions are not going to change the world, but you have no choice but to make a decision anyway. Which side are you going to be on? Righteousness or something else? Generosity of spirit allows you to persevere and that seems to me one of the most powerful messages or lessons of the Dharma.

The Karmapa

This is a big question. We all have hopes for change in education and the environment, for example. This is especially true for the youth. The discussions that eventually became this book were dialogues with university students from the United States. They all had a strong wish to move things in a positive direction and the courage to try and change themselves. Usually, in wanting to make a shift happen, when we are looking outside of ourselves, we are losing a lot of time trying to create a movement for change. Actually, hoping to alter the way other people think is not the most important thing. We need to look inside and see how much we can change ourselves.

In terms of gender issues, we have had numerous discussions about education and full ordination for Tibetan nuns. One can have long talks about external changes, but the main thing is that the nuns transform themselves. Their motivation and way of conducting themselves are key. From one perspective, external conditions do have an influence, but the main thrust here is that the nuns need to work through their sense of inferiority, develop confidence, and find fresh hopes. What energizes this change is a powerful wish for transformation, belief in themselves, and courage.

Professor Davis

That brings up my next to last question. In the book, the word *courage* often appears. "The basic fact of my interdependence is a source of courage and determination." "Courage is the root of compassion." "A great deal of courage is needed to keep our minds and hearts open." "Compassion is accompanied by courage in order to come to its full force in the world." I found the word coming up throughout the book. And it speaks to your last comment — that it takes courage for an individual to be responsible for their spiritual transformation. Am I right in that? Is that what you mean by "courage"?

The Karmapa

I think so. When we speak of courage in the context of interconnection, it means that since we are all interrelated, we have a responsibility for each other. There is also an emotional connection that links us together; since we all can feel pleasure and pain, we can experience compassion for one another. This is not a question of philosophy, but a connection through feelings that we all share, so it is not a heavy thing. Actually, compassion and courage are very similar: to be compassionate, we must be courageous and invoke our capacity for dedication and joyous involvement. It is only when we can do this that we will be able to truly benefit others.

Professor Davis

I want to thank you for the opportunity to be with you and thank the audience for its patience. I have traveled a great deal in Tibet and one cannot be but worried about the future of Tibetan civilization when one experiences what is happening on the ground in Tibet. I do not want to get into a political conversation, but when one hears the Fourteenth Dalai Lama speaking about the possibility that he will not be reincarnated and this might be the end of his lineage, what does this mean for the future of the entire Tibetan Buddhist contribution to civilization? It has given so much to the world. If it were not for the Tibetans, we would have lost all touch with the Buddhist teachings in India after the Mogul invasion.

This repository of knowledge, scholarship, and wisdom

seems to be so fragile because of the geopolitics of today. Are you hopeful that the Dharma will continue to grow, to inform, to inspire, and to give spiritual comfort to people throughout the world?

The Karmapa

In general Tibetans regard the Dalai Lama as their sole hope, refuge, and protector. What this has meant in actuality is that individual Tibetans do not take enough responsibility for their own lives, but shift it onto the Dalai Lama. When he passes away, then, in whom will we place our hopes? We cannot imagine that and many do not even want to consider it. The reality, however, is that some day it will happen though we do not know when.

You mentioned Tibetan civilization and this really depends on the Tibetan people. The best situation would be if they could create organizational structures to preserve it. In India and other countries, actually right here in Canada, there are many Tibetans who could establish these associations. In terms of Tibetan Buddhism, there are quite a few young leaders who have wisdom and knowledge, and I think they will develop well, but it will be difficult to find a universal leader like the Dalai Lama.

At this point, the questions were opened up to the audience.

The first question concerned how to deal with the political situation in the world and particularly in the United States. What view should we have in relating to the various situations that come up?

The Karmapa

I am watching contemporary politics very carefully and we have new news to watch every day. On the one hand, we can look at leaders and see how much change they can bring about in the outer world; on the other hand, we can look at ourselves and see how much change we can bring about in our inner world. We need to know our own capacity to transform ourselves.

It is difficult to know the future, and in the present we see a continual stream of news that focuses on unsettling events. Our brains are drowning in them so we need to pull ourselves out of this situation, think for ourselves, and open our minds to a fresh outlook. This is critical. We are submerged in an unceasing flood of news, and politicians use that immersion to influence and shape our minds. We need to look at both sides.

The second question was from someone who suggested that the Karmapa spend a portion of the rest of his incarnation training as many young girls and boys as possible in the same way he was trained, so that when his lifetime would come to an end, no one would have to go looking for the next Karmapa — Karmapas would be everywhere.

The Karmapa

What you say is true. The name Karmapa means "a person of action" or "the one who carries out the activities of all the buddhas," and so forth — there are many ways of explaining it. In brief, the name refers to the buddhas' deeds or activities to benefit others, and a person who does that is a Karmapa. As I mentioned earlier, at a young age I was told that I was the Karmapa before I could decide for myself. From one perspective, whether or not I am the Karmapa is not important. From another perspective, it has given me the opportunity to make connections with other people and to benefit them. That is how I think of it. Actually, not only myself, but everyone has this opportunity to become the Karmapa. If everyone acted like the Karmapa, that would be very good, and also, I would have a lot less work to do.

The third question was from a young man who asked about self-control. In the West, it can often mean suppression and rigidity, whereas in the Buddhist monasteries he visited in India, there was a sense of flow and freedom along with self-control. How can Westerners learn this?

The Karmapa

When we talk about the freedom that comes from self-control, there is a tendency to think of it in terms of being strict with oneself. We look at ourselves from the outside and feel that we have to be firm and on guard, and not risk losing control. Actually, what we are talking about here is more relaxed. As I mentioned before, we need to find a harmonious way of relating to our emotions. In terms of your question, we are looking at tension and relating to it with a sense of spaciousness to open the tension up. We could give ourselves more opportunities to experience this open, spacious feeling, and that will counteract the tightness and release the tension of being too hard on ourselves.

Relevant here is how we understand the concept of self. Buddhism often speaks of "no self" or "the nonexistence of the self," but this does not mean a complete and absolute negation of self. We negate the small self; however, the vast, universal self does exist. It is the constricted, narrow self caught in a slim realm of thought that does not exist; the vast, spacious, and universal self does exist. We could give ourselves more opportunities to experience this wide-open space.

We come to our knowledge through our personal experience.

The Karmapa

Chapter Ten
Working with Disturbing Emotions
The Practice of Akshobhya

To look at how can we deal with the powerful emotions that arise in our minds, it would be good to start out with an introduction to the Buddha Akshobhya. In the Buddhist teachings, and especially for those who are practicing in the Mahayana tradition, there are the buddhas of the ten directions. In addition to Shakyamuni Buddha, the one most of us know, there are all the buddhas in the many realms of the ten directions. These are individuals who have realized perfect and complete awakening just like the Buddha Shakyamuni.

Far beyond many oceans of worlds, the Buddha Akshobhya resides in the pure realm of Abhirati (*mngon dga'*, "Delight") to the east. The name Akshobhya means "imperturbable" or "unshakeable" in Sanskrit. Before becoming a buddha, Akshobhya was a bodhisattva who made great aspirations or commitments, and among them, the greatest was his vow: "From now until full awakening, I will not allow the feeling of hatred or anger toward any

living being to arise in my mind." Since he was able to firmly maintain this commitment and never wavered, he was
called Akshobhya or the Imperturbable One.

His name is related to his special commitment not to
become angry. He made great efforts to uphold it over a
long arc of time, clearly showing what a courageous spirit
he had. All of us can take him as an example for how to
work with our afflictions. In our daily lives, we deal with a
range of emotions, provoked by internal and external conditions. Of these two, the most challenging are not our
external problems, but our inner emotional conflicts,
which are the most difficult to handle. In Buddhism, we
spend long hours studying and researching the afflictions,
and practicing how to apply the antidotes to them.

When discussing how to remedy the afflictions, first we
have to clearly identify the character of a particular affliction and then examine how it affects us. We should also
investigate it to find out whether it is harmful or beneficial. We study a specific affliction carefully and come to
know what it is like, and only then will we be able to
deal with it. Otherwise, not knowing its nature, we will be
caught up in the affliction and it will overpower us.
Forcing the situation and blocking the affliction is not a
solution that will work.

Normally, when we talk about afflictions in Buddhism,
we focus on three — greed, hatred, and ignorance in their
various aspects. Some of these are easy to recognize and
others more difficult, so we have to be patient and take
time to come to know them. Over the years, we have

become so accustomed to the afflictions that they reside within us as familiar habitual patterns, and we usually lose ourselves to their control. So we need a special awareness that can see the state of our mind, which normally we do not pay much attention to. To counteract the afflictions, we familiarize ourselves with the emotional weather patterns moving through our mind.

From my own experience, I know that it takes time to work with the afflictions and to clearly recognize one of them takes four to five, maybe even ten years. During these years we are not just passing the time of day, but training ourselves, investigating with mindfulness our behavior and actions. We are posting the lookout of mindfulness to see how the afflictions arise. Usually we do not do this, so anger, for example, suddenly takes over before we have time to think about it. But when we set up a sentinel to keep watch, our mindfulness will develop gradually. We can begin to see the causes and conditions for anger and the phases in which it manifests. All of this will give us more time to deal with it.

It is important that our understanding of causes for the afflictions is based on our own direct experience. Someone else explaining them or talking about what happens from their point of view will not help us, because this remains a mere understanding. We need the immediate, raw experience of the emotion so that we can clearly identify it. We come to our knowledge through our personal experience, which is the only way we can apply an effective remedy.

Akshobhya's commitment relates to all of the afflictions,

but mainly he vowed to refrain from anger. This was why he was named the Imperturbable One. I would like to give some advice related to how we can apply an antidote to this challenging affliction.

Some years ago I took a great interest in everything related to Akshobhya and his practice, and translated from Chinese into Tibetan the *Akshobhya Sutra*, which had not previously existed in Tibetan. This process of being immersed in the translation created a deep connection with Akshobhya, so that his life story became connected with my own emotional state at the time. I had came to India at the age of fourteen and faced many complex and problematic situations, so it was difficult to let my mind rest naturally or peacefully, for it was often disturbed. Sometimes when things were not going well, I was easily angered and my temper flared. I knew that getting angry was not a good thing, and yet when such circumstances arose, I could not stop it from happening.

This was the situation in which I began research about Akshobhya. When I saw the great aspiration that he made not to let anger appear, I felt, "Ah, this is directly connected to where I am now," and thinking it would be good to imitate him, I made a stronger effort.

In these modern times, how is it that we see Akshobhya? Usually we feel that he is a buddha residing in a remote realm at a vast distance far away from us. Yet when I thought about the aspiration he made, I had a new feeling or insight, a sense that another method was possible. I thought about his commitment not to get angry from the moment he aroused bodhichitta until full awakening. When we think of our situation, could we make the commitment not to get angry for one single day from morning to night? Do we have the confidence we could do it? Would we have the ability to do it for a week? Thinking in this way can shift our perspective.

We could debate about whether we are able to refrain from anger, but instead of debating, it would be better to try and see if we can actually do it. Sometimes we say, "Oh, I couldn't possibly do that," and just give up. This is called the laziness of putting yourself down, which is the worst of all types of laziness. Instead of this, we should step up and challenge ourselves to see if we can do this or not. Can I refrain from anger, if not for a day, then from early morning to noon? And how about from noon until evening? We will not lose anything by simply trying.

Saying, "I'm not going to get angry" is easy to do when things are going well and we feel comfortable. However, when problems put pressure on us or create causes for anger, such as something unpleasant sitting right in front of our face, that is when our minds get disturbed and we learn something. You could say that we have a positive person and a negative person within us: one says, "I'm going to get upset and angry," and the other says, "I'm not going to let this get to me." Usually, we go with the first person, who wants to get angry, and rarely do we let the second one prevail. The problem here is that our stance against anger is not strong enough; our position is weak and so we are overcome. When we can give one hundred percent control to the part of us that does not get angry, only then will we be able to counter anger in a difficult situation when it appears with all its fiery energy.

We need to establish a firm position, based on clearly knowing what our aim is and the path to it. Beyond this, we should be rather strict in our allegiance to our goal and not let our mind just wander off wherever it wishes. We stick to our plans along with the aim we have set for ourselves. Following our guidelines, however, we shouldn't become too rigid or too serious, for in doing so, sometimes the affliction gets even more serious, so we can be a bit playful, too, and more relaxed. Things will work out better this way. We try, and if it does not work out, we try again.

Generally, teachings about disturbing emotions are very personal. Before in Tibet, each disciple would spend years in an individual relationship with their teacher, who would gradually give commentary and instructions related specifically to them along with personal advice. Now we have had only a short time to talk about the affliction, and I hope that some of it has been beneficial. Tomorrow we will continue and look at other methods for working with the afflictions.

Instead of focusing on an object that seems to be out there, we should turn inward and look at the conscious subject.

The Karmapa

Chapter Eleven
Putting the Teachings into Practice
Questions and Answers

When practicing mindfulness, we can set a goal for the day and then track what happens to see if it turned out the way we had planned. Previously in Tibet, practitioners would examine themselves inwardly to see if they could rely on an antidote for their afflictions or not. If they were successful, they put out a white stone, and if not, a black one. This gave them a graphic image of how they were doing. Was the antidote working or not?

For them, this practice felt like play that they enjoyed and we could follow their example of not being so overly serious. While we are working with the afflictions, we could also be open and in a good mood. This intention is important as it creates the atmosphere of a relaxed mind that is joyful and more spacious.

When applying an antidote, we become like two people, one positive and the other negative. We must firmly decide which one to follow, for if we do not, our minds will waver and easily change. In this unstable state, it is difficult to remedy the afflictions with any success. Once we have decided which side we will follow, we should often remind ourselves of that commitment. If we do not, at some point our decision will slip away. Decisiveness, courage, and dedication from the depth of our being will allow us to sustain our resolution.

Sometimes I imagine that it would be helpful if we would record our resolution on a device that would automatically play our words back to us when we were faltering, so we could hear ourselves making this promise. What often happens is that once we have resolved to do something, we are unable to apply the mindfulness and carefulness needed to maintain it. Our minds are captured and distracted by outer appearances, so we gradually forget what we wanted to do.

To develop our mindfulness, we could examine the state of our mind every three hours for three months and remind ourselves this way. After three months, even if we are not so perfect about checking our mind, we will have gradually created a new habit.

Now it would be good to have some questions and answers. Generally, people come to ask me a wide range of questions, some of which are major and others are rather minor. Due to all the work I have, it's not possible to answer them all, and actually, I think if we really look, we can eventually find the answer ourselves. For example, in his younger years, the Buddha was curious, seeking to know the truth about birth, old age, sickness, and death. He asked questions and looked within himself for the answers, eventually he went forth, leaving his home to learn what he wanted to know. Likewise, it is good to train and search for our own answers to the questions we have, because in going through the process of seeking to know something, we actually learn a lot. It is difficult to say how much we learn in just asking and receiving a response.

Questions and Answers

When seeing important teachers, people sometimes experience attachment, anxiety, and fear. Resentment and anger can arise around these situations and that can be difficult. What can we do?

When we Dharma practitioners encounter a difficult or challenging situation, it should not be seen as something external to ourselves. Instead of looking outward at "an obstacle," we should look inward and see the connection to our mind. This allows us to recognize everything that appears around us as our mind's magical illusion. Further, we can understand that in any given situation, people will have different ways of seeing, and we will esperience a variety of perceptions. Our minds project in myriad ways depending on the different habitual patterns we have.

It is important to remember that what we see is not something coming at us from the outside, but rather our mind's projection shaped by the imprints within it. This is the way we should regard all these situations. If we think that what appears arrives from the outside and then focus on it as a separate object, we are creating a false distance, which then produces hopes, fears, and suspicions.

Therefore, instead of focusing on an object that seems to be out there, we should turn inward and look at the conscious subject.

From this perspective, difficult circumstances are actually an opportunity to learn something and improve ourselves by applying the antidotes for afflictions. This is the motivation we should bring to problematic situations.

When practicing mantras or what you have taught us, how do we do so in a way that brings us deeper into the teachings? And secondly, how do we remain close to you even when you are far away?

To respond to your first question, the source of mantras is linked to what are known as *den tsik* (*bden tshig*) or "true words." These can be explained in two ways. First they can be seen as relating to the way things truly are, in other words, the abiding nature of phenomena. Secondly, they can be seen as words of plain-spoken truth, as expressions that are not false. Mantras relate to this second description.

The mantras we recite are related to a particular deity, for example, Avalokiteshvara. From the time he gave rise to bodhichitta, he made vast aspirations to benefit living beings; he firmly maintained his commitment without wavering, so he did not deceive others. Reciting his mantra reminds us of his trustworthy motivation. Most mantras are related to the names of the deities, so they represent the courage, the mental strength, and the unwavering commitment of that being. It is important that the mantras have this deep connection, because when we come to recite the mantra, we are not just repeating mere words; the mantra has a history and a background, and when we know this, the mantra can impart its special power.

In response to your second question, in order not to feel separated from the teacher no matter how far away they might be, the main practice is to train in embodying as many as possible of the qualities in the teacher's mind — their compassion, loving-kindness, and so forth. The more we develop these qualities, the closer we come to the guru. It is strange that sometimes when someone is far away, we have the feeling of their being quite close, and when they are close by, there's a feeling of distance. The feeling of being close or far does not really depend on physical proximity or distance. It is also true that we have met many times in the past and hopefully we will meet many times in the future.

I have a problem with anger. When it comes, I stop caring about commitments, about others and myself. I feel as if there are walls around me and I'm separate from everyone. Another problem with anger is that it appears so quickly that I can't see it coming. It jumps out from nowhere and takes over. How can I see it coming and stop it before it takes a grip on me? And if it does take over, how do I free myself?

There are two approaches. One is applying our mindfulness, awareness, and carefulness to know what is going on within ourselves, and this keeps us from being overwhelmed. Anger can come on abruptly. If you know how to swim, for example, and suddenly fall into a lake and panic, you can forget how to swim. So it is important that we continually work with being mindful, aware, and careful.

In the course of our lives, we all have become angry many times, and when we look back on those incidents, we can see that we seem to have transformed into a different person. When we get angry, we are transfigured into a frightening person. If we think about our mind at that time, it is as if it had mutated into an alien, someone very different from whom we normally are. All these times that we got angry in the past were losses for us and we do not need to augment them. We can, however, learn from them by looking at the downside of anger and its faults, and thereby coming to recognize anger for what it really is.

The second part of your question had to do with the speed at which anger occurs. Here, being mindful, alert, and careful helps. Sometimes there is a warning that anger is coming; you have the feeling, "Uh-oh, this is not going to go well. I'm about to get angry." And other times anger comes abruptly. It is immediately full blown in the very next second and we have no time to think between these two moments. Before we go on a rampage, it could help to flash on a memory of what our teacher advised, "My wise lama said not to get angry." It is also true that we get angry when something unpleasant happens that we do not want, so it could help to bring up something pleasant and delightful instead. It might not completely change the anger but this shift could dampen it.

If we work with being mindful, alert, and careful, we will come to see that anger is actually a process that arises in stages, and this gives us the opportunity to stop anger before it becomes fully manifest.

A few months ago, I had a fear that my lama would not be with us for long, and this fear continued to grow stronger and spread to other areas where I was not fearful before. It has come to the point now that I'm afraid of the fear itself. How to I regain clarity?

It is easy to talk about this, but in actuality is difficult to face this kind of challenge. I can say something, but I think it is quite challenging to deal with this emotion of fear. One way to work with the fear of losing your teacher is not to focus on the external teacher, but the internal one. The scriptures speak of an outer spiritual friend and an inner one. The former is the one who teaches us the Dharma. If we are skilled in meditation, the latter one is the practice that has matured in our own mind. All the positive things within us that our lama has taught are experienced as a significant presence or a certain sense of being weighty. Actually, the word *guru* comes from the Sanskrit root *gru* meaning "heavy" or "weighty." We can place our trust in this inner teacher, which will give us a certain independence. Our internal lama becomes a place to which we can turn for refuge, and then we will no longer feel lonely, empty, or fearful. So it is important that we do not rely only on an external guru for teaching, but build up our internal guru as well. Over time, our own mind becomes a refuge, in which we can place our trust and our hopes.

Our teacher has given us so many priceless living jewels,

but somehow they get lost, and when we search, we cannot find them. We should save these jewels within our mind and come to trust them as points of reference, a resource that we can rely upon. When this trust develops, we can rely upon what has become an integral part of our own mind.

My concern is about taking a vow that we then break. Last night you spoke of taking the vow of not getting angry, which could be difficult to keep. Would you please address this fear and then talk about what to do when we realize we have broken this vow?

It is important to know that here we are not talking about pratimoksha or bodhisattva vows with all their precepts to keep and possible failings. In the case of working with anger, "vow" might be too strong a word. To put it simply, we are just trying. And if we cannot do it, then we try again. If we lose once, then we try ten more times. If we lose ten times, we try a hundred times. We can think of the afflictions as not being so heavy or onerous, for it is important not to lose heart. If we fail, we can deal with it and carry on. Being courageous and not becoming discouraged are key. So this situation of working with anger is different from the pratimoksha or bodhisattva vows and their precepts. Here, we are just trying to see what works.

What about this situation? There are two guys and a third one is behind them. This third one knows the other two and is totally free. When I can be in touch with him, I try to stay that way but it is not easy. Can you talk about this third guy and how to stay with him?

Maybe that third guy is you. Imagine that you are standing between two advisors who give diametrically opposed feedback; one of them gives you good advice and the other bad. Sometimes politicians are faced with a similar situation. Which advisor we chose to follow is crucial. Usually, we listen a little bit to one and a little bit to the other, but in this way, what we truly need does not become clear.

What we should do is look at our own mind. We can listen to both the advisors if we know what we basically think. Otherwise, things will not go well if our own mind is uncertain and we listen to one or the other of the advisors. First we have to know what we think and need, and then we listen to an advisor. If their words harmonize with what we know, we take in what they say. In sum, we have to make our own decisions based on knowing our goals and knowing what we think and need. Advisors cannot make the decisions for us.

I have a question concerning your teaching last night about the practice of Akshobhya. When people's minds are not so stable, conflicts come up. If we talk with someone and do not get angry, is that the same as being patient? Previously in Bodh Gaya Your Holiness said that if we do not respond to people who harm us, that in itself is harmful. There are also teachings on the practice of vajra anger. What should we do?

Generally, getting angry is not difficult; it is not getting angry that challenges us. In Mahayana and Vajrayana texts, there are discussions about taking anger onto the path, especially in the Secret Mantra. These explanations, however, assume that you already have control over your afflictions and that loving-kindness is your primary motivation. If this is not the case, taking anger as the path will be very difficult.

As beginners, we should apply the antidotes for the afflictions, especially patience, the remedy for anger. We should study and practice the remedies, for in this way we will gradually develop and finally be able to take the afflictions as the path.

I work for a nonprofit that educates parents about how to reconnect children with nature and also to reconnect within the families themselves. We ask them, for example, if they could spend one hour together without looking at their screens. We also let them know that the radiation from the screens is harmful during the long hours children spend looking at them. However, people do not want to hear our message and sometimes I struggle to find the skillful means.

All the digital devices that fill our lives have stolen a lot from us, including our mental happiness as well as our connections to each other and to nature. At the dinner table, the members of a family do not speak to each other but send around text messages. Our feelings and experience of each other are negatively affected and so is our connection to the place where we live. For example, where I grew up in Tibet, we had a rich and powerful feeling for our homeland. But for city dwellers, their homeland can be a room or an apartment in a tall building where they can go for ten years without speaking to their neighbors.

Not only are they not relating to the human beings

around them, they also have lost their connection to nature. It is not like that for Tibetans. When you say "homeland," it evokes images of mountains, valleys, and rivers — a whole natural landscape. These days, people spend so much time with their digital devices that their minds shrink and they become lonely and depressed for lack of real connection with other people and the natural world.

So there's a difference in the way we bring up and educate our children. I think it is also important to spend time in a natural environment, and even cities have parks. The main thing is to keep our spirits up and not to become discouraged. If we can inspire others and ourselves, that is the best.

Acknowledgments

It is always a delight to thank the people who have made a project possible. First, the two translators, Tyler Dewar and David Karma Choephel, have spent decades in service to the lamas and the Dharma. We see them mainly on stage, yet behind the scenes they are doing so much more. Thanks go to them for all the hours they have given. This book began in conversation with Beata Stepien, and as she has done for years, Yeshe Wangmo proofed the text and added excellent suggestions. Maureen McNicholas also contributed helpful feedback and created a beautiful design for the book. Karin Lucic gave a careful and astute read to the final version of the manuscript. May the resulting text repay their generosity in benefiting an ocean of readers.

Resources

Books by or about the Seventeenth Karmapa, Ogyen Trinley Dorje

Celebrating the Karmapa: Remembering His Kindness. Tr. Lama Yeshe Gyamtso. KTD Publications: Woodstock, NY, 2010.

A Collection of Commentaries on the Four-Session Guru Yoga. Compiled by the 17th Karmapa Ogyen Trinley Dorje. Trs. David Karma Choephel, Eric Triebelhorn, *et al.* Kagyu Monlam and KTD Publications: Woodstock, NY, 2017.

Compassion Now. Tr. Lama Yeshe Gyamtso. KTD Publications: Woodstock, NY, 2011.

The Dance of 17 Lives: The Incredible True Story of Tibet's 17th Karmapa by Mick Brown. Bloomsbury USA: New York, NY, 2005.

The Dharma King: The Life of the 16th Gyalwang Karmapa in Images by the Gyalwang Karmapa, Ogyen Trinley

Dorje. KTD Publications: Woodstock, NY, and Altruism Press: Sidhbari, HP, India, 2016.

First Karmapa: The Life and Teachings of Dusum Khyenpa. Trs. David Karma Choephel and Michele Martin. A Karmapa 900 Publication published by KTD Publications: Woodstock, NY, 2012.

The Future Is Now: Timely Advice for Creating a Better World. Tr. Ringu Tulku Rinpoche. Hay House: New York, NY, 2009.

Heart Advice of the Karmapa. Trs. Tyler Dewar, Karl Brunnhötzl, *et al.* Altruism Press: Sidhpur, HP, India, 2008.

The Heart Is Noble: Changing the World from Inside Out. Trs. Ngodup Tsering and Damchö Diana Finnegan. Shambhala Publications: Boston, MA, 2014.

His Holiness the XVIIth Gyalwang Karmapa. Tr. Michele Martin. Karma Lekshey Ling Publications: Kathmandu, Nepal, 1992.

Interconnected: Embracing Life in Our Global Society. Tr. Damchö Diana Finnegan. Wisdom Publications: Boston, MA, 2017.

Karmapa 900: Ebook. 3rd ed. Karmapa 900 Publications and KTD Publications, Woodstock, NY, 2017. Available from KTDpublications.com.

The Karmapa: Urgyen Trinley Dorje by Ken Holmes. Altea Publishing: Forres, Scotland, 1995.

The Karmapas and Their Mahamudra Forefathers by Khenpo Sherap Phuntsok, tr. Michele Martin. Wisdom Publications: Boston, MA, 2016

The Miraculous 16th Karmapa: Incredible Encounters with the Black Crown Buddha by Norma Levine. Shang Shung Publications: Archidosso, GR, Italy, 2013.

Music in the Sky: The Life, Art, and Teachings of the 17th Gyalwang Karmapa, Ogyen Trinley Dorje by Michele Martin. Snow Lion Publications: Ithaca, NY, 2003.

A Ngondro for Our Current Day by His Holiness the Gyalwang Karmapa. Trs. Tyler Dewar and David Karma Choephel. KTD Publications: Woodstock, NY, 2010.

Nurturing Compassion: The First Teachings in Europe. Trs. Ringu Tulku Rinpoche and Christophe Klonk. KFE Publications: Brussels, Belgium, 2015.

Traveling the Path of Compassion: A Commentary on the Thirty-Seven Practices of a Bodhisattva. Trs. Ringu Tulku Rinpoche and Michele Martin. KTD Publications: Woodstock, NY, 2009.

His Holiness the Karmapa on the Web in English

kagyuoffice.org — The official website of the Karmapa

karmapacanada.org — The Karma Kagyu Association of Canada, organizers of the Canadian tour

kagyu.org — Karma Triyana Dharmachakra, the North American Seat of the Gyalwang Karmapa facebook — Search for "Karmapa Ogyen Trinley Dorje"

kagyumonlam.org — The yearly prayer festival under the Karmapa's guidance in Bodh Gaya, India

rumtek.org — Website of Rumtek Monastery in Sikkim

kagyutv.org — Live webcasts and an archive of selected videos

Karmapa on YouTube — Look for "Karmapa Ogyen Trinley Dorje"

Aryakshema.com — Winter Dharma Gathering for Kagyu Nuns

dharmaebooks.org — Free ebooks of classic Buddhist texts and teachings in several languages.

khoryug.org — A network of Buddhist monasteries and centers in the Himalayas working together on environmental protection

The Main Centers and Associations that Hosted the Karmapa in Canada

Great Compassion Bodhi Prajna Temple, 19 Hidden Forest Dr., Cedar Valley, Ontario LoG 1EO. Resident teachers are the nuns Miao Jing and Miao Yin. www.gcbptemple.org

Karma Sonam Dargye Ling, 12 Maynard Ave., Toronto LoG1Eo. Canadian Seat of HH the Gyalwang Karmapa. The resident teacher is Lama Tenzin Dakpa. www.ksdl.org

Karma Tashi Ling, 10502–70 Avenue, Edmonton, Alberta T6H 2E9. Under the guidance of Khenchen Thrangu Rinpoche. The resident teacher is Ani Kunsang. www.karmatashling.ca

Karma Tekchen Zabsal Ling, 13900 Leslie Street, Aurora, Ontario L4G 7C8. Under the guidance of Khenchen Thrangu Rinpoche. The resident teacher is Lama Tashi Dondup. www.ktzl.org

Palpung Yeshe Chokhor, 75 Nipissing Road, Milton, Ontario L9T 2P2. Under the guidance of HE Tai Situ Rinpoche. The resident teacher is Lama Karma Phuntsok. www.palpungtoronto.com

Rigpe Dorje Centre, 503, 5e Avenue, Verdun, Quebec H4G2Z2. Under the guidance of HE Jamgon Kongtrul Rinpoche. https://rigpedorjemontreal.org

Thrangu Monastery Canada, 8140 No.5 Road, Richmond, BC V6Y 2V4. Under the guidance of Khenchen Thrangu Rinpoche. The resident teacher is Dungse Pema Tsewang. thrangumonastery.org

The Tibetan Association of Alberta, 2339–16A Street SE, Calgary, Alberta T2G 3T3. www.albertatibetan.org

The Tibetan Canadian Cultural Association, Gangjong Choden Ling, 40 Tutan Rd., Etobicoke, Toronto, Ontario M8Z 2J8. www.tcccgc.org

Dates and Places

Chapter One
Love and Compassion Are Critical to Our Lives
Calgary, Alberta, Canada
June 14, 2107

Chapter Two
Transforming Disturbing Emotions
A Dialogue among the Three Major Traditions of
Buddhism
Convocation Hall, University of Toronto, Toronto,
Ontario, Canada
June 1, 2017

Chapter Three
Ground, Path, and Fruition, Session I
Enercare Centre, Toronto, Ontario, Canada
June 2, 2017

Chapter Four
Ground, Path, and Fruition, Session II
Enercare Centre, Toronto, Ontario, Canada
June 2, 2018

Chapter Five
Finding Freedom through Meditation
Enercare Centre, Toronto, Ontario, Canada
June 3, 2017

Chapter Six
Compassion Is More Than a Feeling
Karma Tashi Ling, Edmonton, Alberta, Canada
June 13, 2017

Environmental Impact Statement

In fulfillment of His Holiness's wish to protect the environment and minimize our eco footprint, as a "green publisher," KTD Publications is concerned about the future of the world's endangered forests and committed to the responsible use of natural resources. When possible, our books include an environmental audit conducted by our printers, which quantifies environmental impact and benefit due to printing processes, ink, paper, and transportation choices for a given publication.